SHE CAN'T BE HER

VANDANA

BookLeaf Publishing
India | USA | UK

Presentation by *BookLeaf Publishing*

Web: www.bookleafpub.com
E-mail: info@bookleafpub.com

ISBN: 9789369547852

First edition 2025

To my family—your constant love, support, and faith in me have been my biggest pillar of strength.

ACKNOWLEDGMENTS

I have written this book with my heart, and I have lived each of these characters. I have felt each word of this book before writing it. It is not a mere story; it is a piece of my experience, feelings, and imagination.

I would also like to take this opportunity to thank all the people who encouraged me during the writing process. My family, who is always there for me, supports each of my choices, and believes in me—your belief in me is my biggest strength and inspiration.

A huge thank you to those who heard me out, offered me criticism, and assisted me in making this book better. Your feedback and advice have been incredibly helpful along the way.

I am also grateful to be publishing my first book, and to the editors who assisted in getting my story ready for its publication. Your feedback has helped to bring this book to life.

This book is for all those who never lose hope and keep pursuing their dreams with determination and courage.

With love,
Vandana

PREFACE

Some wait to pile up with years—no promises, no expectations… just a pain that remains in the heart. This is the tale of one such wait—a boy who, for fifteen years, waited for a girl he knew for only seven days. He has everything—money, popularity, a life almost perfect—but there is a void in him that no one and nothing can fill.

And then she returns.

But for clarity, he has confusion. The woman he dreamed of all these years is standing in front of him now, but his emotions toward her no longer seem as effortless as they once were. The surety he held onto begins to disintegrate. As secrets unfold, the meaning of his wait turns entirely different, revealing things he never anticipated.

I wrote this tale because storytelling is my strength, my identity. I always believed that a wonderful story was not just a string of words—it's a feeling that settles deep within the heart. This is not just a love and wait tale, but one of feelings that change over time and reveal to us unexpected realities.

If you've ever stood waiting for someone with no guarantee, if you've ever lost yourself in your own emotions, then perhaps this story will sound familiar to you.

–Vandana

CHAPTER 1

It was nightfall. I rested on my bed, gazing at the ceiling. I possessed everything—a posh penthouse, a career that thrived, fame, and riches—the sort of existence people only wished for. Earlier, even to me, it had been an aspiration. However, when it turned into a reality, I understood that pure bliss existed far away from all this.

Honestly, this world remained a fictional movie to me. The individuals around me were speaking as if they had a pre-written script to read out loud—pretentious, filled with artificiality. No true attachment or bond with anybody existed. Everything was like an ornately decorated novel, and I was merely acting my part in it.

But a certain part of me was also stuck in the past and refused to move on. I still felt the lack of someone—a space I knew could never be filled. But even then, my heart would not let go. Maybe because those moments, those memories, were so lovely and valuable that I could spend my whole life in them. Those were my true memories—warm, genuine, and mine. And then, there was my current life—barren, lifeless, as if someone else had scripted it for me.

That evening, the suffocation was intolerable. The never-ending wait, the loneliness that would never subside—it all sat within me like an immovable burden.

That sense of missing someone with every fiber of your being yet being unable to do anything about it. That sense of helplessness, of pain. Perhaps nothing was crueler than that. There had been someone in my life who had provided me with the loveliest of memories but also left me with a never-ending wait.

I recalled sitting on the riverbank, observing the sparkling lights reflect off the water at night, feeling the chill wind on my skin—it was the only thing that ever brought me calm. It was the only thing that ever made me feel alive. But in the never-ending chaos of life, I had lost even that.

I shook off my mind and stepped out of bed. I had to go out, to breathe.

I picked up my black hoodie, donned a mask, and exited my room. As I made it to the living room, my eyes dropped in front of me, and I froze.

Alex was my manager for seven years, but above that, he was my best friend. He lived in my penthouse with me, and his presence was a quiet reminder that I wasn't completely on my own in that world. No matter how crazy things got, he was there—a steady, unshakeable presence. In the ocean of new faces, Alex was the only one I felt was home.

He was sitting at his laptop, totally lost in the virtual world that seemed so expansive and impersonal. In this strange new world where everyone had a mask on—either literally or figuratively—there was one individual who did not bother to hide behind a mask. That individual was my boss, my best friend, and possibly the only person who cared for me for reasons other than fortune and fame.

The moment he heard the creaking of my footsteps coming down the stairs and into the living room, he didn't instantly look up. His fingers just kept on typing, his gaze on the screen. But then, after a moment's hesitation, he looked up at last, and his face clouded over. I pushed my hands deep into my hoodie pockets. "I'm taking a walk."

His scowl grew more pronounced. "You know that's a gamble, don't you? The paparazzi are in full force. If someone spots you, it'll be on the internet tomorrow."

I knew he was correct. I had taken years to be cautious, always keeping the facade, shying away from unwanted attention. But at that moment, I didn't care.

"I'll be okay," I said, gritting a weak smile.

Alex had most likely read my face. He understood that even though I occupied myself, loneliness existed someplace deep inside me, one that disturbed me.

"Ethan, are you okay?" There was a thread of concern in his voice.

"Yeah, I'm fine."

But that was a lie—a lie I told every day for years. I was tired of saying it. Just once, I wished I could say—*No, I'm not fine. I am shattering into pieces on the inside.*

But my lips never mustered enough courage to speak those words. I pulled my hood up, pulled my mask over my face, and plugged my earphones. "I'll go now?" I raised an eyebrow.

He smiled and returned to his laptop.

"Listen, call me if there's any problem."

But I was already out the door before he could get another word out.

The night air wrapped around me like an old friend, cool and clean. I strolled through the deserted streets, the city humming in the background—the faraway blast of a car, the cadenced steps of late-night stragglers, the muted buzz of neon lights. Music enveloped my ears, creating a bubble around me, cocooning me in the type of isolation I had been craving.

Night quiet enveloped me as I went away from the road, sinking my legs deep into the yielding grass. There was a faint breeze in the air, and with each stride, it seemed as if I was leaving it all behind—as if the bank of the river before me called out to me, offering release.

The moon's light played on the water's face, the silky ripples running as if possessing a heartbeat of their own.

Something had registered when I came near.

On the ground, leaning up against a bench, was a dark shape.

At first, I assumed it would be another vagrant who had stumbled from exhaustion. But when I approached the figure, something didn't feel right about the scene.

There were forgotten bottles of liquid littered along the bench, and the glass in each reflected the pale illumination. There was crumpled bread scattered across the floor, and a tattered wrapper balanced on the verge of falling over on the bench.

A worrisome tension crept up my spine. My heart began to pound slightly—most certainly not because I was frightened, but for some reason I could not articulate.

I stood still for a moment.

Should I just leave?

And then, as if some unseeable force was drawing me, I crept down by the figure.

Long hair swept across the face of that woman, obscuring any view. I attempted slowly to roll it over.

And that's when I knew—

It was a woman.

I let out a small gasp as a tidal wave of something unexplainable washed over me.

Her skin was white; her breathing was shallow.

My fingers shook as I reached out once more.

Why was I behaving in that manner?

Who was she? And why was she lying here like that?

I was about to do something else when the clatter of running footsteps whirled me around.

A young woman came running toward us.

Her face reflected no panic, no evident emotions—just quiet determination.

She knelt beside the unconscious woman and softly patted her cheek.

"Mam… Mam, can you hear me?"

Because there was no answer, she looked at me, her eyes scanning my face.

"Help me?" Her voice was demanding but panicked. "We have to get her into the car."

I didn't delay.

Gently, I picked up the unconscious girl in my arms. As soon as I did, I felt a peculiar sensation wash over me—a dizzying, unpleasing feeling that sent shivers coursing down my spine.

My hands were icy. My heart raced frantically.

I didn't know why.

I had no idea who she was.

But there was something about that moment that was important.

The other girl, though, was calm.

She was on the phone now, talking in a casual, sort of bored voice.

"Yes… I've found her. I'm bringing her now."

That was all she said before she hung up.

I scowled.

There I was, a stranger, oddly disturbed by that unconscious girl—and that woman, who was with her, didn't seem to care.

Why?

We got to the car. She opened the door and gestured for me to load the unconscious girl into the backseat. I did so at once.

She climbed into the driver's seat.

She closed the door. Turned the engine on.

And before I could say a word, the car disappeared into the evening.

I was left standing there, the wind still blowing through me.

But here, there was turmoil.

"Who is this girl? Why am I feeling worried about her?"

1st June 2006

Like every year, we have come to Lushbrook again. But this time, something is missing. Justin—my big brother—is not here with me. It has been ten months, yet his lifeless body still haunts my vision. No matter how much I try, I can't escape it. I miss him so much.

Mom and Dad stay busy, and before, it never really bothered me because Justin was always there. But now, our house feels empty, almost suffocating. Silence has turned into something eerie—sometimes I hear strange noises that aren't really there. But Lushbrook brings a little peace. Grandpa, Grandma, and Uncle are here. Even if it's just for seven days, I feel a bit lighter.

Today, my Uncle and I went to buy flowers. I sat outside the shop, lost in my thoughts, my eyes heavy with unshed tears. Then, out of nowhere, I noticed a group of kids my age. They were laughing together, sharing candies. One boy, who was handing them out, caught my gaze. Instead of eating the last candy himself, he walked up to me and placed it in my hand before leaving with his friends.

It was such a small thing. But for the first time, someone gave me something without me asking, without me giving them anything in return. At school, I was always the one sharing my snacks with my friends. This moment should've been insignificant—but I can't seem to forget it.

Maybe, just maybe, kindness still exists in the world. And maybe, I am not as invisible as I thought.

CHAPTER 2

The morning air was cool; the sky still shrouded in darkness as I emerged from my penthouse and walked to Alex's apartment. I rapped—firm, but not brutal. Hard enough to rouse him.

"Wake up. We're leaving."

Nothing for a few moments. Then, a muted rustling noise came from inside, followed by the creaking of the door slowly opening. Alex leaned in the doorway, his hair disheveled, his eyes half-open. He rubbed his face with a hand, grimacing.

"It's five in the morning," he grumbled, squinting at the clock on the wall as though expecting it to be lying.

I dismissed his complaint. "Get ready. We leave at six."

He stood in the doorframe, arms crossed. "Why do you go there every year?"

I didn't respond. I wasn't up for explanations.

"To see my parents," I said at last.

"Right. But why the same day, the same time, every year?"

My fists clenched a little. I breathed slowly. "Don't ask questions. Just get ready."

He paused a bit before he went in, looking at my scarf strangely.

"Why do you always have it on when we go there?"

I pulled at my scarf. "I like it."

"It's 40 degrees Celsius outside, man. You're crazy."

He closed the door of his room and I stood there, patting my scarf softly with a smile. There were memories I associated with this scarf, but how could I ever try to explain that to Alex? This scarf was never given to me by anyone, but someone had worn it, and since then, it has become special to me. Just by their touch, the scarf carried their fragrance, which I could always feel.

We got into the car as the first light of morning crept over the horizon. Veridale's streets were quiet, the city stretching out in slow motion. Alex was behind the wheel. I sat quietly, observing the world whizzing by the window, my thoughts elsewhere.

June 1st. Each year. Seven days. Lashbrook.

It wasn't a tradition. It was an unwritten rule.

Alex was familiar with the routine by now. He didn't press for information, just simply turned on the radio. A gentle, mellow melody hummed in the background, filling the silence.

Lashbrook was the sort of town that seemed untouched by time. It was situated between mountains and rivers, its valleys filled with wildflowers, the air heavy with the smell of pine and wet earth. It was quiet. Peaceful.

My parents resided there, in a house on top of a hill. From their porch, you could watch the sun set behind the mountains, coloring the sky in gold and crimson.

As we arrived, I got out and breathed deeply. The air here was different—cleaner, fresher, with something almost nostalgic.

My parents greeted me with smiling faces as I entered our little but comfortable house on the hill. Although small in size, the house had a stunning view of the valley below, where yellow fields stretched on and on and faraway mountains rose high above the horizon. The fresh air carried the smell of wildflowers, making the location even more peaceful.

We sat at the wooden dinner table for a hasty breakfast, exchanging frivolous chatter in between bites. My mother baby-talked over me, checking that I had enough to eat, while my father laughed good-naturedly at her typical spoiling. Alex, sitting snugly next to me, was one of the gang. He'd been visiting Lushbrook with me for the last seven years, and my parents had grown to love him. They teased and joked together, making jokes about marriage and dating, with Alex gladly going along. Occasionally, he would glance over at my father, sharing a knowing look as if plotting to humiliate me even more.

Alex sat at his computer, completely absorbed in the cyber world that was so vast and anonymous. In this bizarre new world where everybody wore a mask—either literally or metaphorically—there was one person who didn't go to the trouble of wearing one. That person was my boss, best friend, and arguably the sole person who loved me for reasons beyond wealth and fame.

The instant he heard the creak of my footsteps descending the stairs and into the living room, he did not look up at once. His fingers continued to type, his eyes fixed on the screen. Then, however, after a pause, he finally looked up, and his face darkened.

Following that family moment, I took my dad's bike keys and set out with Alex. It was something I did annually, and Alex knew it well. He had been accompanying me to Lushbrook for the last seven years, and every turn, every path of this journey was as known to him as it was to me.

Lashbrook roads were narrow but familiar—scrawled on my mind like the creases of an ancient map. I led Alex through twisting streets, by places that felt like home.

"You already know where we're headed, don't you?" I whispered.

Alex released a sarcastic smile. "Of course. I've been going there with you for seven years."

I slowed the bike to a stop. "Stop here."

We stood in front of an imposing mansion—regal, spotless, its white facade shining in the gentle morning sunlight.

We never entered. We merely observed. Waited.

Every year, a fleet of shiny black cars pulled up. Doors slid back with ease, and one after another, immaculately attired silhouettes emerged—wealth clinging to them like a second skin. They nodded to each other, smiled graciously, and then melted into the mansion.

But my gaze hunted for only one face.

And she wasn't present.

A familiar pain clenched in my chest.

"You've never explained why we visit here," Alex spoke softly.

I kept my eyes glued to the entrance of the mansion. "I'm waiting for someone."

Alex put a firm hand on my shoulder. "Why don't you go in and ask?"

I had done all that before, countless times. I had asked about her innumerable times, but I never received a proper answer.

Alex sighed. "Ethan, these people are ridiculously wealthy. Are you sure it's worth waiting for someone who probably doesn't even remember you?"

His words should have hurt. But they didn't.

Because I had felt the same way a thousand times.

She was like a princess.

And I was nothing compared to her.

But still, I remained there. Every year. With hope, when there was no longer hope to be found.

Call me Izzy. Only those who are closest to me use that nickname.

Her voice lingered in my head, unaffected by time.

Alex let out a frustrated breath. "We're going to the river next, aren't we?"

"No. Take me home. We'll go there tomorrow."

Alex clenched the handlebars. "Ethan, don't get mad, but... it's been fifteen years. I don't think that person even remembers you."

He was right.

She had never promised to come back. Perhaps I should have realized she never would.

She had never tried to reach out. Perhaps I was just a distant memory.

After all, we had only spent seven days together.

Seven days.

Maybe that was all they were to her—merely seven brief days.

But to me, they were everything.

And no matter how many years went by, I couldn't let them go.

I went back each year.

Hoping she would as well.

But just like every year previously—she never did.

And yet, some obstinate piece of me just couldn't bring myself to stop waiting.

5th June 2007

I saw that candy boy again today.

I was strolling along the river when the candy boy suddenly caught up with me. Not uttering a word, he knelt down and fixed my loose shoelaces. Then, as fast as he had appeared, he dashed off.

In a world full of people who think only about themselves, there are still individuals who assist others without wanting something in return. He was such a person. His little deed reminded me of something my brother used to tell me:

"Many will be your friends because you belong to a rich family. Be cautious while selecting them. Those who remain with you without paying attention to your wealth are not common. Never let such individuals go."

And now, I knew I had to search for him.

The previous year, after that encounter near the flower shop, I had returned numerous times with the hope of catching another glimpse of him—but I never succeeded. I had no idea about his name, either. Now, I was left with a single day more before I could depart.

Would I ever spot him again?

CHAPTER 3

I sat at the rear of my house in Lushbrook, observing the darkening night sky. The coolness held a sharp sting to the night wind, but some sort of lethargy was settling within.

She never did show that year either.

I had hoped, hoped that after losing her parents a month ago, she would come back here, to the only place that had ever been home to her. But she hadn't even gone to their funeral. Had she never come back at all, not even then?

"Hey, what are you thinking?"

Alex's voice snapped me out of my reverie as he settled next to me. He stretched out his legs, cocking his head slightly to look at me before adding nonchalantly, "By the way, is that Izzy we're after?"

I snapped around at him, shocked. "How do you know her name?"

"You never told me the secret behind that big house," he said, a smirk tugging at his lips. "So I asked your mother." Then, leaning in, he added, "She said the girl from that house was your friend."

A lump formed in my throat.

I looked away, my fingers curling into my palms. Izzy. I had never spoken about her to Alex. How could I? How was I supposed to explain who she was? Why do I still come here every year?

Alex studied me for a moment before teasing, "Look, either you tell me, or I'll tell your parents that you come here every year and hang around that house like some lovesick fool."

I glared at him. "Don't you dare!"

He chuckled, relaxing back. "Then speak up."

I breathed in deeply, my throat dry, as I watched the sun lower on the horizon.

I brushed a hand through my hair. The night air chilled my skin, sending a shiver down my spine.

"The girl I've been trying to find... Her name is Izzy. We met fifteen years ago."

Alex's eyebrows rose in surprise. "You've been searching for her for fifteen years?" He laughed briefly. "I thought you never attached yourself to anyone. Is that your grand love tale?"

There was a sadness in my eyes, but a very faint smile curled on my lips.

"Come on, come on. How did you date her? And why did you and she break up? If she dumped you, why are you still searching for her?"

His questions came at me like bullets, but I stalled. I knew that if I explained the truth—that I had only met Izzy for seven days—he'd never let me live it down.

I gazed upwards at the sky. The clouds were streaked with the dying golden rays of the sun, their edges lit against the deepening blue. The wind held the distant rumble of the river.

"The first time I saw her was here."

My tone softened, memories sweeping over me.

"It was raining. She must have been lost."

Alex did not say anything, just listened.

"We brought her inside the house to help her. That is how we met and we became friends."

"It seems short, by the way. How long were you two friends?" he inquired.

"Seven," I said.

"Seven… years?" He appeared astonished. "You mean, childhood romance?"

I shook my head. "Not years."

His brows knitted. "Seven months?"

I sighed and shook my head once more.

His jaw went slack. "Seven… days?"

I didn't answer. I just turned away, knowing full well how absurd it sounded.

Alex's face fluctuated from incredulous to amused. He took a step back, regarding me as if I'd gone mad.

"Wait—so you've been visiting here for fifteen years due to a seven-day friendship?"

I remained quiet.

"Is this madness?" he grumbled to himself.

Alex rubbed a hand over his face, then laughed and shook his head. "Man. You're crazy."

Then, in exasperation, he waved around us. "Seriously? We do this same thing every year for… that? Seven days? That wasn't even a real friendship!"

I gulped. "You're right. I don't know why I'm still searching for her."

Alex shrugged, folding his arms. "Were you in love with her or something?"

I paused, "Maybe I was... Maybe I still am."

But the truth was, as I waited for her, with every passing year, my affection for her grew. And the memories we had shared did not wear off but became stronger.

"Come on, Ethan," Alex complained, holding me by the shoulder. "That was nothing. Just a brief encounter. You can't waste the rest of your life brooding over it like this."

"It ended when she left," he said, speaking in a gentler tone as if attempting to reach me.

The day I last visited her, she approached me... silently.

She handed back my scarf—just that. Nothing else.

And then she just turned around and went away. Silently.

No farewell. No promise of another meeting. No expectation of tomorrow.

It seemed as though she was ending all things... as if I never meant anything at all.

Alex released a harsh breath, running his fingers through his hair. "Ethan, wake up. The world is enormous—you can find someone else." He moved back, giving me a side glance. "I'm telling you, that was nothing. Even if she does return, I don't think she'll remember you. You're the only one still clinging to it."

Some of his words were forcing me to think.

What if he was right?

What if she didn't remember me?

What if she refused ever to have known me?

What would I do in such a situation?

Would my heart be able to bear it?

7th June 2007

What a strange coincidence! I saw him riding his bicycle right as we were leaving Lushbrook for Veridale.

It has been three years. Every year, I go there, hoping that this time I will finally get to meet him properly, but every time, it ends the same way—an unfinished encounter. I spend the whole year thinking about this moment, making plans, yet everything slips away.

Now, I'll have to wait another long year—once again, returning in search of that familiar yet unknown face. But this time, no matter what happens, I will definitely meet him next year.

CHAPTER 4

We came back from Lushbrook. I sat on the riverside, blending into the solitude of the night. My hood was pulled over my head, my mask concealing most of my face. No one paid attention to me. To them, I was just another shadow among many, a fleeting presence in the quiet expanse of the riverside.

The air was crisp, carrying with it the distant hum of the city, the occasional laughter of strangers, and the rhythmic hush of the wind as it skimmed over the water's surface. The river flowed with silent persistence, untouched by the noise of the world, and for a brief moment, I felt at peace.

And then—an odor.

A pungent whiff of alcohol sliced through the tranquility, shattering my stillness. I turned my head instinctively, my senses immediately alert. And there she was—the same girl from that night.

She sat beside me, as if that bench belonged to her, as if she had been there all along, waiting. Her posture was careless, yet something was haunting about the way she sat—something too at ease, too accustomed to that kind of solitude. The dim light from a distant streetlamp outlined her disheveled figure. She held a loaf of bread in one hand and a beer bottle in the other.

I watched in quiet confusion as she dipped the bread into the beer and took a bite.

She wasn't drinking. She was eating that bread while dipping it in beer.

A strange discomfort settled in my chest. The scene before me felt too odd, too unsettling. She wasn't just another reckless drunk drowning her thoughts in alcohol—there was something deeper, something painfully habitual about the way she did it.

I turned my gaze away, back to the river, pretending I hadn't noticed. But curiosity, or perhaps something more than that, took hold of me. The silence between us stretched, but the questions in my mind did not quit.

Before I could stop myself, the words left my mouth.

"You shouldn't drink outside like that. It's dangerous to your health."

My voice was even, devoid of judgment, just a passing observation.

For a moment, nothing changed. She paused mid-chew, her movements coming to a halt. Even the sound of her quiet chewing disappeared, swallowed by the space between us.

Then, slowly, as if my words had reached her from across a great distance, she lifted her gaze and met mine.

And in that moment—everything stopped.

The city, the river, the world around us.

Her eyes—those eyes—froze me in place.

A sudden, inexplicable weight pressed against my chest. My heartbeat faltered, then quickened, the rhythm uneven, erratic. Something ancient and aching stirred within me, a force I couldn't name.

The way she looked at me wasn't just recognition—it was something deeper, something wordless yet deafening.

I felt like I had been dragged into a storm of memories I didn't even realize I had forgotten.

A warmth spread through my body, yet at the same time, a hollow, aching void opened inside me. My vision blurred, and to my own disbelief, tears burned at the edges of my eyes. But why?

Why was my heart pounding as if it recognized something my mind didn't?

Why did her silent gaze feel like an ocean of unspoken words, memories buried beneath layers of time?

I felt exposed, as if she had stripped me down to my very soul. Every unspoken word I had ever locked away, every feeling I had buried—it was all there, staring back at me in her eyes.

I couldn't look away.

I didn't want to look away.

The more I searched her face, the deeper the ache inside me became. It was maddening and heartbreaking.

I was unraveling, and she—she was the cause of it.

Who was she?

The intensity of the moment held me captive. I wanted to speak, to ask, but my lips remained frozen. My thoughts were tangled, slipping away like sand through my fingers.

And then—she did something unexpected.

Without a word, she lifted the beer bottle and handed it to me.

She didn't hesitate. She didn't explain.

She simply placed it in my hands as if it belonged to me, as if that was always meant to happen.

And then, before I could process anything—she stood up and walked away.

She didn't turn back.

She didn't say a single word.

She simply faded into the darkness of the street, disappearing like a ghost, leaving me frozen in place—still holding onto the bottle she had left behind.

I swallowed, the weight of her silence pressing into my chest. My fingers curled around the glass, gripping it tightly as if it held the answers I so desperately sought.

The air around me felt colder. The river continued to flow, oblivious to the storm raging inside me.

What the hell just happened?

In a matter of minutes, a storm had brewed within me.

Who was she?

Why did she seem so broken?

And why did a single glance into her eyes leave my heart so painfully heavy?

I didn't know what it was about her, but the moment she was gone, she had taken something with her—or perhaps, she left something behind in me.

I simply sat there, still clutching the bottle she had put into my hand, and my thoughts kept coming back to one thing—

"Who is she? And why did I feel that way?"

11th August 2007

Today, while I was sitting by myself in my room, I was filled with sadness. Since Justin passed away, I've felt so isolated. Then, I saw Sophia standing there. She was attempting to comfort me; her presence was a weird but comforting heat. Even during the most somber moments, she has a way of making me laugh.

She's fun, she's cool, and she's an extrovert—but she also possesses a temper. She knows how to stick up for herself... and for me, just like my brother used to. She's nothing at all like me, but at the same time, she's the only person who feels like she really stands with me.

CHAPTER 5

Mr. Smith and I were engrossed in a discussion of the subtleties of a scene we were to shoot soon when Alex showed up, a bit out of breath, walking purposefully toward me.

"Hey, Ms. Robert is wondering if you're available that weekend for dinner," he said nonchalantly, but I detected the undercurrent of curiosity in his voice.

Ms. Robert was a very gifted woman. Gorgeous, successful, nice—someone who possessed an effortless elegance that people were drawn to. Her being was radiant, the kind that made you feel noticed, heard, and valued. She had invited me out to dinner before—more than once, really—and each time, I avoided giving an answer. Not because she wasn't worthy of my attention, but because I couldn't force myself to say yes.

The reality was plain: I couldn't afford to raise someone's expectations falsely.

One shouldn't be made to wait for something she could never be given. And I… I had nothing in my power to give her. My heart was already taken years ago—handed over by someone who'd left without knowing what she was leaving behind. Someone who had carried with her every aspiration, every tenuous hope I ever cherished.

She wasn't returning.

And still, the passion that I felt for her remained pure, unpolluted, untainted by the passage of time.

That was not a love I could transfer or reform into something else. It was not something I could impose upon another story, another woman. It was hers—had always been hers. To look for fragments of her in another would be cruel—not just to her memory but to the woman I would inevitably compare her to.

I sighed, already knowing the response I would provide.

"No, Alex," I whispered, my voice softer than I intended. "Tell her I thank her for the invitation... but I won't be able to attend."

Alex let out a deep sigh, his annoyance barely hidden. "Because of Izzy, maybe?"

He sat down next to me, pulling out a chair. The instant he did, Mr. Smith stepped back, quietly excusing himself from the discussion. He knew. He had witnessed that before.

Alex leaned forward, his voice dropping as if that would hurt less. "Ethan, how long are you going to remain like that? How long are you going to let a ghost keep you from living? Move on."

His words hung in the air between us, heavy and unyielding. But rather than responding, a small smile played on my lips—not from amusement, but from quiet resignation.

Move on? I told myself, more or less. From whom?

From one who was never mine to start with. She hadn't stormed off from a fight. She hadn't reneged on a promise. There was no betrayal, no leftover bitterness, no unresolved words between us. She hadn't disappeared after making a vow to come back. She hadn't stormed off from me after saying, "I love you."

That was how I felt, and I didn't blame her for it.

I was the idiot who had remained stationary, expecting something that was never destined to be.

She never knew.

She never realized that in the silence between words, I had committed to memory the curve of her smile when she thought she was alone. She never realized that I had clung to the sound of her laughter, the way her voice gentled when she talked about things that were important. She never realized that whenever she turned away, part of me wanted to call her back.

But I never did.

Because that love was never going to be shared by both of us. It had only ever been mine.

It was a love that had grown in silence, in the recesses of my heart where words unspoken resided. A love that had never had the opportunity to breathe, to live outside the delicate walls of my mind. And yet, it was everything.

"Tell me, Alex, how do you move on from something that never was?"

"How do you release what was never yours to begin with?"

I didn't know.

"You're wasting your life, Ethan," Alex said at last, his tone softer now. Less angry. More… sorrowful.

I faced him, with the only truth I had left to give.

"I know."

And perhaps that was the most terrible part of it all.

I knew.

I knew, and still, I couldn't release her.

12th December 2007

My grandparents came to see me today. Everything was as usual at first—Grandma brought me my favorite cookies, and Grandpa inquired about school as usual. But then the talk turned into something I wasn't ready for.

They informed me that they were sending me to Eldoria for more education. A good school, better prospects, a brighter future—that's how they explained it.

But deep within, I had known the real reason—they were sending us off to Eldoria because Sophia and I had become too much of a problem for school. Our presence was getting to be too much, and they didn't want it to reflect on Grandpa's career as a politician. That was why they had decided to exile us.

Not because it was best for us. Because their reputation mattered.

CHAPTER 6

Alex and I arrived at the Grand Regent Hotel, and as soon as we stepped inside, Alex's eyes lit up admiring the place. The hotel was every bit as luxurious as you'd expect from the Thorntons. Marble floors gleamed beneath the crystal chandeliers, and the grand lobby was buzzing with an air of wealth and sophistication.

As we walked further in, I heard a familiar voice call out from behind. I turned around and saw Mr. Andrew Thornton approaching, surrounded by four people. He looked just like I remembered—confident, with that casual charm that ran in the Thornton family. His father, Richard Thornton, owned the Grand Regent Hotels all over Astravia, and Andrew was the younger son, clearly being groomed to help run the empire after his elder brother's death.

"Hey, Ethan! It's been a long time. How have you been?" Andrew greeted me, extending his hand.

I grabbed his hand firmly. "I'm good," I replied.

"What brings you here?" he asked with genuine curiosity.

I told him about the meeting I had scheduled, and he nodded. "Well, Lumia's film's 25th-anniversary party will be held here; I'll see you at the party then." With a polite smile, he turned and headed off with his group.

As we continued walking, Alex couldn't help but ask. "Wait, was that Andrew Thornton? How do you know him?"

I didn't feel like explaining and I never wanted him to know about that, so I kept it short. "Yeah, he is Izzy's uncle."

Alex gave me a surprised look. "She is from the Thornton family!"

I didn't say anything and just kept moving, and before long we were on the 12th floor where Mr. Smith was waiting for us. We greeted each other and took our seats around the large conference table.

Mr. Smith didn't waste a single moment. "I have made some changes to the script, so I thought we should go over them."

Before we could get into the details, Alex interrupted. "Where is Ms. Arden?"

"She's coming."

Julia Arden was my co-star for the movie, and as beautiful as she was talented.

After a few minutes, the door opened, and Julia entered. She was wearing an elegant green dress with short hair and an expensive designer bag on her shoulder. She greeted everyone with a warm smile and sat down beside me.

"You're even more handsome in person," she said, smiling.

I gave her the same compliment out of politeness. Julia turned heads everywhere she went, but to me, she was just another actor I'd be working with.

Mr. Smith began reading through the script changes, but I could feel Julia's eyes on me the entire time, making me a little uncomfortable. I ignored it and focused on the conversation at hand. Once the meeting was over, I excused myself and headed outside to clear my head.

I began looking for Alex. I called his name when I saw that girl from the riverside. She was still wearing the same clothes. She looked about as confused. I walked toward her. “Do you need any help?”

She looked at me that day with an expression different from the one of yesterday, showing a kind of arrogance that I had not seen yesterday. I couldn't help but think that maybe the advice I gave her last night hadn't sat well with her. Perhaps she didn't appreciate it as much as I thought. I tried to say something, but she turned her back on me completely.

Julia looked puzzled. “Do you know her?”

I shook my head. “Not really.”

Julia smiled and asked if I wanted to join her for dinner, but before I could answer, my phone rang. It was Alex, sounding urgent. “Ethan! Come to the stairs, quick!

I rushed over, Julia following behind, and when we got there, Alex was pointing at a small tree. “Look at that! It's incredible!” It was rare and exotic, tucked away in a little garden by the stairs. He was completely fascinated by it.

“Alex, get the car,” I said, tying up loose ends as I could feel the day's weight pressing down. I glanced back at Julia, who was standing a few steps away from me, unreadable on her face. “I'll see you later,” I said, looking for a flicker of anything on her end.

She nodded, but there was a distance in her gaze that I couldn't quite decipher. With a final wave, I turned and headed out from the Grand Regent, the familiar grandeur of the hotel looming ahead. The air felt cool against my skin, a stark contrast to the warmth of the conversation I had hoped to continue.

As Alex pulled the car up, I was about to get in when I saw the girl again, standing near the entrance. I asked Alex to stop the car and got out. Walking up to her, I offered, "I can give you a ride if you need it."

She shook her head, an ironic smile playing at the edges of her lips as she pointed to a car nearby, one that I hadn't even noticed—sleek and expensive. Her whole attitude had changed. The bewilderment I had seen in her eyes was gone. Instead, an arrogance of confidence now spread across her face, as if she enjoyed the show, her tone dripping with a telltale superiority.

"Why bother with anything less?" she said, her voice laced with a hint of mockery.

Alex's jaw dropped when he saw the car. "Oh my god, who is she?"

I glanced at him, a hint of a smile creeping onto my face. "That's the drunk girl I ran into by the riverside."

Alex shook his head, still disbelieving. "She looked like a mess, but that car! It's like night and day."

And then he said something that gave me pause.

"By the way, that is the first time you've cared about someone other than Izzy."

I stared at him, a little bewildered myself. There was something about that girl—something that attracted me to her.

Perhaps Alex had picked up on something I hadn't yet seen. "Come on, man. Forget about her. Give a chance to her."

I had not given her any notice, but in reality, there was just something about this girl that drew me to her. But I would never grant another person Izzy's spot in my heart. That one was going to sit empty, but I was not going to award it to anybody else. And yet somehow I could not rid myself of this girl's memory. I was waiting for the night just so that I could see her, although I didn't even know why.

I went out for my evening jog, and I found myself drawn to the same spot by the riverside once more. I could not explain why, but something about the place had a magnetic pull these days—an invisible force I couldn't resist. Maybe it was the serenity of the water or the way the city lights danced on its surface at dusk, casting a shimmering glow that captivated me, or maybe something else.

But there was something more; I wanted to see her again. She felt familiar, as if there was a connection I could not place. So I stopped by the riverside, my heart pounding with anticipation and confusion.

I stayed there for a long time and also removed my mask. I was just sitting on the bench, lost in my thoughts. As I was about to get up, suddenly, she appeared again—the girl. Without saying a word, she sat right next to me, just like before. There was an odd silence between us. She was eating bread, casually sipping from a bottle of alcohol.

And the next thing, she was sitting beside me when suddenly all that was pent-up inside of me started to break out. Then, at that moment, just by her presence beside me, I could sense that feeling, that unutterable sense between us. I was really in love with that girl. God, no way.

Was it just a momentary confusion, or was I misreading my feelings? The moment that thought crossed my mind, I dismissed it. How could I think like that? That girl was a mess.

But still, my heart, I felt at that moment, said something different to me. An invisible pull, something that seemed to attract her, which cannot be ignored. Maybe it was just a mere feeling, but in that split second, my heart was screaming at me not to, for I couldn't possibly be drawn to her.

"Have we met before?" I asked, my voice softer than I had intended, as if I were afraid of what she might say.

She gets up from the bench with the fluidity that defies her slenderness and takes one step closer. My heart beats into an erratic rhythm, throbbing faster when she bends into me. Her hood casts part of her face into shadow. All her long hair spills forward in a frame, which makes it impossible to look anywhere else.

"You have grown even more kind," she whispered, her voice soft yet charged with something unspoken, her eyes locking with mine for what felt like an eternity.

And just as suddenly as she'd closed the distance between us, she turned and walked away, her departure as mysterious as her presence. I stood there, frozen, her words echoing in my mind like a haunting melody.

"Could it be her?" That thought initially crossed my mind, but the next second, "She can't be her. How could I even think like that? Have I lost my mind?"

31st May 2008

Tomorrow we're off to Lushbrook. But Sophia's not coming—I've made sure of it. I'm not going to risk her making a scene, not when this journey is so important to me. This is not just a visit; this is my final opportunity before departing for Eldoria.

I've been looking for him for three years. My candy boy. I don't know if he remembers me at all, but I remember everything—his smile, his voice, the way he brightened my world a little bit. It's probably foolish to hold onto a memory like this, but my heart won't let it go.

If I don't find him this time, will I ever?

Hoping for a miracle. Hoping for him.

CHAPTER 7

The cameras of the media flashed incessantly as I arrived outside the Grand Regent Hotel. The 25th anniversary celebration of Lumia's film had drawn an impressive crowd, with countless big names from the industry. As I stepped inside, the sheer grandeur of the event was breathtaking—chandeliers glittered above, and the hall was abuzz with conversations and laughter, packed with familiar, illustrious faces.

And then, we reached him—Richard Thornton.

He stood tall and commanding, his silvered hair combed back, his tailor-fitted suit exuding an air of old-world wealth. He was not just a businessman or a politician preparing for the presidential election; he was a titan who had shaped industries and lives.

The moment he saw me, though, his face changed. He opened his arms wide and took a step forward as if welcoming me into a world that felt both familiar and daunting.

He embraced me warmly, without any hesitation. It was not the usual polite handshake or distant nod. It was real. For a moment, I forgot about the crowd around us.

"How are you, young man?" Richard asked, his voice deep but full of affection, as if we hadn't just seen each other for years.

"I'm good, Grandpa. How are you?" I replied, my voice quiet, a hint of something more personal slipping through.

As soon as I called him "Grandpa," the air in the room seemed to shift. The noise around us softened, and I could feel eyes turning in our direction. Whispers started circulating among the guests. I could almost hear their thoughts: How does he know Richard Thornton? Is he really his grandson?

But we had a life beyond that heredity, and I was in no way ready to tell it in a room full of people I didn't even know.

Richard didn't flinch at the attention, giving a gracious smile to those around him, and reached out to touch my shoulder. "Good to see you here."

I smiled back at him. I was accustomed to his presence, but something made me ask, "Where's Grandma?"

He gestured toward the grand staircase, and my eyes followed his pointing hand. And there, at the top of the stairs, was Margaret Thornton. She stood tall, moving gracefully in the soft gray dress that flowed so beautifully with each step. Even now, at 70, she seemed to hold an ageless beauty, a quiet strength that somehow seemed far younger than the years told her to be.

Without a thought, I moved toward her, my feet carrying me up the stairs as if drawn by a force I couldn't resist. As I approached, her face lit up, her warm smile stretching across her lips.

"It's been too long," I said softly as I reached her. She opened her arms, and I stepped into her embrace, feeling her familiar warmth surrounding me.

She held me for a moment, then pulled back slightly, her hands resting on my shoulders as she looked at me with a mixture of pride and tenderness. "It's been five years since I last saw you," she whispered, shaking her head slightly. "Why did you stop visiting us?"

I nodded, guilt washing over me. "I'm sorry, Grandma. Work's been… overwhelming."

She smiled softly, brushing a stray lock of hair from my forehead. "I know, my dear. But I'm proud of you. Proud of what you've accomplished. You've grown into such a remarkable young man."

Her words struck me harder than I thought. I swallowed hard, finding my voice to ask the question that had been plaguing me since I got here. "Izzy…w…where she…" I started, but a familiar figure appeared at the top of the stairs before I could finish.

We walked in to greet Eleanor Thornton, Andrew's wife. She comes with a good-practiced smile toward us. Then she said softly, tapping Grandma's arms, "Time to join everybody else, Mother." Her sense of timing proved almost too coincidental. A part of my mind was suspicious that she got in just right when I'd been about to ask the one single question that had hounded me for years. Eleanor nudged her down the stairs, into the crowd.

I stood there for a moment, watching them disappear, feeling the question I never got to ask in the air between us.

Alex appeared beside me, his hand going to my shoulder once more. "Come on," he said softly, nudging me back toward the party. "There are still a lot of people you need to meet."

But my mind was no longer where it belonged. It was with the silent question and the odd sense that something else was at work—something I wasn't being told.

Alex stood by the bar, swirling the wine in his glass, his eyes fixed on me. His gaze was steady, curious, but there was something more beneath it, something questioning. I noticed it almost immediately, and after a moment, I couldn't help but ask.

"What's going on?" I said quietly, stepping closer to him. "Why are you staring at me like that?"

He paused for a moment and then decided that he should at least say something. He put his glass back toward his mouth so he could continue drinking the wine before locking my gaze again. "Why were you calling Mr. Richard Thornton your grandfather? He is Izzy's grandfather."

It hung there between us, suspended in mid-air: that question he had posed, laced as it was with the weight of curiosity and confusion. I took a breath of air, the pressure of the truth sitting heavily upon my chest, but I could not bring myself to explain anything to him truly—not now, not here. "Actually, I was…" I murmured, my voice barely above a whisper. "Because I was a friend of Izzy, they asked me to call him grandfather."

Alex furrowed his brow, trying to look past my vague words. His eyes slightly narrowed as he asked gently but insistently, "Oo that."

Just then, I overheard a few feet away where Mr. Andrew Thornton was having a telephone call. His voice was low but full of tension. Perhaps something significant was happening. "Bring her inside," he commanded sharply and ended, then promptly moved over to Richard Thornton.

A chill crept down my spine. Something was wrong. I crept along, silently watching from behind the corner but close enough to hear. "Dad, she's not coming in." Andrew reached Richard that time, quieter but full of anxiety.

My heart stopped for a millisecond. Her? Could be…? Dampness made my hands fall limp, as my pulse started picking up speed before I could turn back, uttering a soft voice, "Is s…she…..is she here?" I paused, taking quick breaths inside my throat for I couldn't keep my steady voice. Each word felt labored with it, weighed to the chest like a burden.

Richard and Andrew just looked at me with faces that said nothing. I felt nakedly exposed and defenseless. Whenever I went to them over the past fifteen years, they never told me anything clearly, and my eyes grew stinging from their imprisoned, unshed tears. I was wildly searching their faces for a good answer in hopes of confirmation.

Mr. Richard Thornton stepped forward with his hand on my shoulder lightly, as if offering me comfort. However, his face was serious. "Yes… she's here," he said softly, trailing off as if there was something more to be said.

I did not want to know anymore. I did not want to be explained or enlightened about anything; just knowing she was here was enough. My heart beat chaotically and my mind revolved. "Where is she?" I whispered out.

Andrew looked around at his father. There was some silent communication between the two. Mr. Richard nodded in silent reply, then nodded to let Andrew speak some more.

Andrew breathed in deeply, his voice low. "She is outside in the garden. Ethan, please don't bring up her parents' deaths and any questions regarding them."

I did not wait for another word. The very moment the words came out of his mouth, I turned on my heel and ran. The world around me became a blur—the grand ballroom, the lights, the music, the people. Everything is all into one big mess, so to speak. All I could see was the pathway through the garden made possible by the mere will to find her.

I ran through the corridors, past the murmurs of confused guests, but their voices were drowned out by the pounding of my heart in my ears. My focus was singular. I could hear Alex calling after me, but his voice seemed distant, like it was coming from another world. Nothing mattered now except the garden, except her.

Tears welled up in my eyes, and at that moment, I couldn't see much of the line of happiness and sorrow. My heart was heavy, and if someone had hugged me at that moment, I would have broken down crying. Everything seemed blurry—the world, the sounds, the people. Nothing was clear. Every beat of my heart was just her. That feeling, the one that stayed with me that whole time. Every corner of my heart was hers, and at that moment, all I wanted was to see her again, to have her in front of me.

I had no idea if she would even recognize me after all these years. Would she still remember me? Or had I become just another faded memory in the corners of her mind? Maybe she had even forgotten my name. Yet, with all these questions weighing heavy on my heart, my steps kept moving forward. Each step carried a mix of hope and fear, but I couldn't stop.

1st June 2008

I finally got to meet him today.

There was heavy rain, and I had lost my way in the woods searching for him. There was thunder in the sky, and I was shivering with cold. For a moment, I felt as if I was not going to make it. The rain pounded against me without any let-up, drenching me completely, and the lightning illuminating the sky only made things worse. My legs were weak, trembling with each step, and just when I thought I couldn't walk anymore, I saw a light in the distance.

Hope.

I staggered toward it, but my feet failed me, and I was going to collapse when I saw someone running towards me. A boy—my age. And then I remembered... it was him.

The boy who had once offered me candy.

He pulled me up, wrapped his scarf around my shoulders, and took me home. He wasn't much of a talker, but the way he was doing things for me said volumes. He ensured that I was safe, warm, and then he escorted me home. Before he left, he pressed a small keychain into my hands—a wee, cute little cat.

I had discovered a friend. A true one. A kind one. One with a good heart. And his name is Ethan Rivers.

Today was the best day of my life.

CHAPTER 8

Isabella Thornton—her name itself sounded like that of a princess. She meant nothing to me but a fantasy—a fantasy that I could see but not touch. Her life was a completely different world from mine—a world of money, extravagance, and influence. Her family was one of the most powerful families in Astravia. Her grandfather, Richard Thornton, was a well-known businessman and politician. They visited Lushbrook once a year on holiday, but their visit never entered my life—until I first saw Isabella.

I still remember that evening clearly. The sky was filled with black clouds, the cold wind howled through the trees, and heavy rain poured down relentlessly. I was sitting by the fire with my father while my mother worked on a woolen scarf. Outside, lightning flashed, and raindrops pounded against the windows. I was busy doing my homework when something outside caught my attention.

A girl… in the rain… trembling with cold.

I blinked, thinking that it was my imagination, but no—she was there. Her golden locks were dripping with water, her clothes clung to her slender body, and she seemed to have been standing in the storm for hours.

Without hesitation, I seized an umbrella and hurried outside. The rain was merciless against my skin, but I did not glance back. As I reached her, I could see how white she was, her lips trembling. I opened my mouth to say a word, but before I could, she fainted.

"Dad!" I shrieked.

My father ran outside and soon realized what was happening. We brought her in together. My mother let out a shocked gasp and rushed to get dry clothes. We wrapped her by the fire, and my mother dressed her in warm clothing before wrapping her in a thick blanket. She opened her eyes slowly after a while. There was something far away in them—a quiet sadness I didn't comprehend. My mother, who had been sitting beside her with worry, offered her a bowl of hot soup. The warm scent of herbs and vegetables filled the air. She took the bowl silently, her small hands encircling it as if to hold its heat.

"I changed your clothes," my mother said gently, sitting beside her. "Yours were wet through."

She nodded slightly, her voice barely above a whisper. "Thank you."

We were in the living room, the center of our home. It wasn't big, but it was warm and snug. A stone fireplace crackled softly in the corner, casting a golden light on the wooden walls. The couch she sat on was old but comfortable, covered in a thick knitted throw my grandmother had made. A small wooden coffee table was in front of her, where my mother had put the soup. Beside the fireplace, my father's worn-out bookshelf leaned to one side, its shelves filled with old novels and a few framed family photographs.

The house was simple, and it had always felt warm. But the girl sitting in front of me did not seem to feel that warmth. She was quiet, staring at the soup as if she had forgotten how to eat. She hardly spoke to my parents, her eyes darting around the room like a lost bird. Every now and then, she looked at me but immediately looked away, as if afraid to meet my eyes for long.

I saw her hands shaking a little, her fingers still white from the cold. Without thinking, I pulled off my woolen scarf—the one made by myself—and held it out to her.

She hesitated for a moment before reaching out. Our fingers touched for a second before she pulled it back, holding the scarf to her chest.

"... Thank you," she whispered again, this time softer.

"I made this, and it's my favorite. Give it back to me later."

I stood there watching her go, wondering who she was, how she ended up there, and why—despite the heat of the fire, the blanket wrapped around her, and the hot soup she cradled in her arms—she still felt so cold.

The moment it ceased raining, my father announced that it was time to take her home. My father worked for her grandfather, Mr. Richard Thornton, and I had heard about the family—rich, influential, and living in the town's biggest mansion. I wished to see it for myself.

"I want to go too," I pleaded.

Father hesitated and then exhaled a defeated breath. "Okay, but be careful."

Over the moon, I got onto the back of his motorcycle while Isabella followed quietly behind him. The ride was quiet except for the whir of the motor and the earthy scent of rainwater. Isabella held on to my father's coat as the wind rushed past both their bodies. Isabella had not said a word since leaving the house.

And then we were there.

I had pictured a big house, perhaps even a mansion, but what I saw before my eyes was more than what my mind could ever conceive.

It was not a house—it was a palace.

Great iron gates with exquisite golden finials blocked our path. Beyond them, there was a long, pavement-stone road lined with verdure, leading to a behemoth estate. The house itself was a work of art—a tall, statuesque, regal white affair, its marble walls glistening under the soft glare of the lamp posts. A stunning fountain dominated the middle of the driveway, water cascading from its several tiers, reflecting the doused light like liquid gems. Luxury cars—long and black—parked close to the doorway, their very presence adding a note of melodrama to excess.

I gasped hard.

This was not a normal family. The Thorntons were royalty in the country.

The moment I walked in with Isabella, I noticed that her grandparents and mother looked worried. Her grandfather was on the phone, calling others to help find her. As we walked in, everyone flocked to her. Her mother started scolding her, but her grandfather stopped her gently and hugged Isabella closely.

"Where have you been, Izzy?" he asked softly.

"Sorry, Grandpa, I made you worry."

"No, no, we were just worried. Where did you go?"

She pointed at me. "I was at his house."

She then quietly walked over to the fountain in the garden and sat down. I kept watching her as her grandfather and the rest of her family thanked me. Then my dad explained to them how I had spotted Isabella and brought her inside.

Her grandfather looked at me and said, "Thank you, son. Tell me, what reward do you want?"

Before I knew what I was doing, I replied, "I want to be friends with Isabella."

His face hardened. "Son, she doesn't talk to anyone outside, let alone be friends with anyone."

I didn't know why, but at the moment, I just wanted to know her. I wanted to see her smile and play with other kids. I had noticed isolation in her eyes, and I wanted to remove it.

"Leave that to me," I said resolutely.

He gave me a small smile. "Alright, if you can change her, even a little, I'll give you any reward you desire."

I rushed excitedly over to Isabella, who was still staring at the fountain. I sat beside her, but she didn't even glance toward me.

"Do you like cats?" I asked, pulling out a cat-shaped keychain from my pocket and extending it toward her.

She looked at me, then at the keychain. "Are you giving this to me?"

I nodded. I didn't even think she'd take it, but she did. A small smile crept onto her face.

"Thanks."

She still looked at the keychain, a smile creeping onto her face. It was probably the first time I ever saw her smile, and it was like seeing a flower open up.

"Do you want to go out with me?"

"Okay."

She agreed so quickly that I couldn't even respond.

Before I could get another sentence out, my dad blew his whistle. It was time to head back home.

"I'll be back tomorrow with my bike. Let's go to the riverbank!"

With that, I sprinted back to my dad, who was still talking with Isabella's grandfather.

Her grandfather looked at Isabella, still smiling as she looked at the keychain.

"Is she smiling?" he asked, as if he couldn't believe it himself. "Yeah, I gave her a keychain. I think she liked it."

A look of hope and relief crept onto his face. Maybe he too believed that I might be able to get Isabella out of her loneliness.

CHAPTER 9

My eyes probed into every corner of the garden, for I had been searching for her for years. Honestly, I had not been able to stop myself from doing so even tonight, when the wait was finally about to end. I walked forward, my heart pounding, and then I saw her—sitting on a bench, staring up at the moon. It was as if she wished to grasp the moon with her hands and hold it close.

I stood up for a while and stared at her, for each memory unfurled like a film playing before my eyes. Was she here in front of me? Or was I imagining her after so long, or was this mere dream waiting to be broken? At that instance, I wanted one thing—one wish only—if this was just a dream, then never, ever wake up.

I couldn't help myself. My heart raced; with me standing behind her, my voice shaking with feelings I could no longer suppress. I breathed unevenly and shouted, "I… Iz… Izzy."

She turned at the sound of my voice. As she slowly turned to face me, I froze in my tracks. That girl I had been meeting by the riverside for the past few days, the one who felt so familiar yet so distant—she wasn't a stranger. She was my Izzy. How had I not realized it? The girl I had searched for every moment of my life, the one I couldn't stop thinking about, had been right in front of me all along.

My heart was full of guilt and regret. I looked down and couldn't face her. "I'm sorry," I whispered.

My voice was heavy, weighed down by all my mistakes. I stood there frozen, my head bowed in shame.

Her eyes became illuminated with a soft moonlight glow, and her smile alone was enough to melt the solid ice around me. She looked into my stare. "Finally, you could recognize me."

"I am… I am sorry; how could I not recognize you earlier?"

She came closer and took both of my hands. The touch was gentle and comforting.

"You recognized me by your heart, Ethan," she said softly. "Your mind just wouldn't let you believe it."

Her words struck something inside of me, and I looked up at her to see the truth in her eyes. She was right. I couldn't ignore her every time I saw her by the riverside. My heart always tried to tell but I refused to believe.

"How did you recognize me?" I asked in a voice barely above a whisper.

She smiled, the soft curve of her lips feeling like sunlight after years of darkness. "When I said I would never forgive, I meant it," she said. Then, she stepped a little closer, her gaze locked with mine.

Her words were breaking down the walls I had built around myself. And then, like a dam bursting, the questions poured out of me.

"If you came back, why… why… didn't you come to me?"

"If you knew it was me, why didn't you tell me?"

"Why did you leave Eldoria without a word?"

"Why didn't you contact me?"

I couldn't stop. The pain of years of longing, the weight of unanswered questions, and the regret of not realizing sooner—everything spilled out. Tears streamed down my face, but she didn't let go of my hands. She just stood there, listening quietly, letting me release everything I had buried for so long.

She raised her hands, soft against my face.

My heart pounded in my ribcage, wild and unrestrained as if it would tear itself asunder. Her touch burned into my skin; her closeness suffocated me with emotions I could not control. Her eyes—God, her eyes—they held me captive, drowning me in their depths.

"Ethan, look at me. And remember this look in my eyes. This is how Izzy looks at Ethan. Never forget that."

Her eyes were a tempest of emotion: love so profound that it felt like forever, pain so new that it felt like forever too, the fear of what could be coming, and something else, something so deep, I couldn't even give it a name.

"I thought… maybe you'd not recognize me," I began, my voice tinged with complaint.

"Why are you crying?" she asked softly.

How could I tell her what I was experiencing? How could I say that this was fifteen years of suffering finally letting go? Every moment of waiting, every sleepless night, every unanswered question had accumulated within me, and now, in front of her, it was all disintegrating.

"Let me cry." I whispered.

"Why?" she asked, her voice hesitant but gentle.

"Please… don't."

She didn't speak; just came closer and hugged me. As soon as she did, I broke apart. A cry ripped through my throat, then another, and I was weeping like a child. My chest hurt, my breathing came in ragged gasps, and my voice, heavy with sorrow, was hardly audible. I couldn't help myself—fifteen years of pain, loneliness, remorse were flowing out of me, melting into the darkness.

Her warmth, the smell of her, the feel of her arms around me—it was home. It was something I had long lost and not expected to recover.

"Can I stop you from crying?" she breathed against my ear.

I shook my head frantically. "No… no no."

She pulled back, though only to have me sit with her on the bench. She sat next to me, near enough that I still felt the closeness of her.

She was looking at me—her eyes, with the emotions she was not verbalizing. Her lips curved with a soft, understanding smile as if she already knew each of the words in my heart that were never being said.

"I was so afraid, Izzy," I admitted on shuddering breaths. "That after all these years, if you returned... and didn't know me."

She smiled faintly, as if my terror was silly, as if she had known me all along. But then she said something that made my heart freeze.

"Why were you waiting for me, Ethan?" While she asked me that, I noticed curiosity in her eyes—she wanted to know something, but...

My throat constricted, making it difficult to speak.

How could I respond? How could I let her in on the truth? That I had been looking for her all these years, not out of obligation but because I couldn't help myself. That she had always been with me, in my heart, in my head, in every breath I breathed.

I covered my face with my hands, swallowing the words that threatened to spill. "I don't know... You just vanished without a word."

Her expression softened. "I'm sorry… I had to go."

My hands clenched into fists. "Will you leave me again?"

Her silence was unbearable. Then, finally, in a voice so quiet it was almost a whisper, she said, "I don't know."

For the first time, I noticed the glint of tears in her eyes. She blinked them away, not allowing them to fall. But before she could respond, her eyes darted past me, her face altering in an instant.

I turned to find her uncle approaching us.

Mr. Andrew.

"I have to go," she exclaimed, standing up. Before I could even think about what was going on—before I could even speak—she took the hem of her flowing dress in both hands and took off. The wind swept her away, her form disappearing before my eyes. I just sat there, staring, not able to make sense of what was occurring. At that moment, it seemed like she was nothing more than a dream—one that was fading away slowly.

She ran around the garden, around the front of the hotel, out of sight down the street. I stood up and went after her, my heart pounding, but she was too quick. Before I could catch her—before I could even yell her name a final time—

A black sedan skidded to a stop.

She pulled the door open, jumped inside, and was gone in a flash—

She was gone.

And I was standing there once again, alone, with more questions than answers floating in my head. Her words continued to echo within my ears. Yet deep inside me, there existed an inexplicable sense of happiness—at least, I got to catch a glimpse of her... and she knew who I was.

A single prayer existed in my heart—please, let this not be a dream.

8th June 2008

Last week was like a lovely dream. I strolled around the whole of Lushbrook with Ethan—he was rather stiff at first, but gradually, he began to unwind. I never gave him back his scarf; I made him a new one with Grandma's assistance instead. But the thing is, I did not want to give him back his scarf. As a token of him, a reminder of these days.

He inquired about next year, but what was I to say? I am going to Eldoria—I don't even know when I will be back. I couldn't bring myself to tell him. I couldn't even properly look at him before I left, nor did I bid him farewell. My heart hurts. After all these years, I had finally found someone I could share everything with. And now, on the 10th of June, I shall depart from Astravia to Eldoria. Yet somehow, I feel that I am leaving something of myself behind.

CHAPTER 10

"Why can't you claim that she loves you as well?" Alex spoke in a relaxed tone while sprawled on the sofa, eating a bag of chips.

I had spent the whole morning discussing Izzy—rehashing every second of last night's party, dissecting each scene, looking for answers. I probably repeated the same questions a hundred times: Did she feel it too? Or was I just another piece of her childhood, an old memory she barely noticed?

Alex, unflappable, barely looked up at me when I leaned forward in my seat, aching for reassurance. But I did not crave a reason from him. I needed him to say, "Yes, Izzy missed you too. She's thought about you all these years, just as you've thought about her."

But no. Not one reassuring word escaped his lips.

When I explained to him that she knew me by the riverbank, he shrugged. "Dude, you're a famous actor now. Anyone would know you."

When I spoke of how she grasped my hand, he grinned. "That's what friends do, man."

And when I swore that I saw love in her eyes, he merely said, "Perhaps it's years of sympathy you're confusing for love."

He said not a word to soothe the tempest raging within me.

And, honestly, a little of me was afraid. What if Alex was right?

What if, in Izzy's eyes, I was still that little boy from a small town—wearing around hand-me-downs, wishing to be someone? Izzy, however, was no ordinary girl. She was a princess at that time, and in most respects, she remained one. From her clothes to her bearing to her aura, there was a sense of elegance that clung to her. She was the sole beneficiary of one of the wealthiest families in the nation. A girl meant for a prince, not for a boy whose dad was an employee of her grandfather.

Why would she ever fall in love with someone like me?

These were the thoughts that nagged at me, but being with Izzy last night had given me an odd sort of peace—a peace I hadn't known in years. But it was laced with fear.

The reality was plain: I loved Izzy. Always had. But another reality dragged me down—What if I didn't mean as much to her as she meant to me? What if she was being nice because she felt sorry for me?

My thoughts circled in a never-ending cycle, knotted in uncertainty. I wanted to believe what I saw in her eyes last night, but doubt stuck to me, refusing to release me.

I sat there, lost in thought, trying to fit all the pieces together when Alex's voice interrupted my silence.

"Okay, let me pop your little bubble of illusions," he said, flinging the half-empty bag of chips onto the coffee table. He sat up, suddenly looking way too serious for my comfort.

"Did she say that she loves you?"

I hesitated, then shook my head. "No."

"Did she say that she missed you?"

Another shake. "No."

His questions eroded my hope, bit by infinitesimal bit.

"Did she say that she came for you?"

I swallowed hard. "No."

"Okay, last one." He leaned in, eyes locked on mine. "Did she say she would contact you?"

I breathed out, the reality crashing down on me. "No."

And like that, my fantasy—one I had been holding on to all morning—broke into smithereens. I dropped back into my chair, feeling as if the world had just flattened me.

Alex clapped a hand on my shoulder; his face smeared with sympathy.

"Come on, man. She's from the wealthiest family in the nation.

Do you really think you matter to her?

To her... you're just someone she happens to know."

As if my heart wasn't already shattered, he chose to tread on the little pieces with his words.

He stood up, disappeared into his room, and came back out with a pile of papers.

"Here," he said, dropping them down in front of me. "That's the script for your next film. Mr. Smith faxed it over. Look at it—maybe more useful than dreaming about Izzy."

I gazed at the script, but Izzy was still stuck in my mind. A movie—possibly a blockbuster—wasn't strong enough to push aside the blender-like chaos within me.

I was still glancing through the pages when Alex pushed his phone into my face.

"See this."

On the screen was a story about Julia and me, discussing our new movie. But Alex wasn't reading the story—he was reading the comments.

"This is what people are saying." He began scrolling.

"Julia and you are perfect together!"

"You guys should totally start dating!"

"Julia is amazing. You're lucky to have her."

I opened my mouth in shock. And he? He just kept scrolling, getting more and more excited by every sentence.

"She's a fan of you, man! And she's fantastic! You have to date her!"

He had talked so much about Julia and me in such a short period of time, but all morning long, not one positive word about Izzy and me had crossed his lips.

Angered, I snatched up the script and gave him a tap on the head with it.

And then, silently, I turned and walked directly to my room.

31st May 2009

I miss Astravia.

I miss Lushbrook.

I miss Grandma and Grandpa.

I miss Uncle Andrew.

And… I miss Ethan too.

If I were present in Astravia today, we would be preparing to head out to Verdile and then to Lushbrook. I miss those days immensely. Sophia is with me, and I'm content with her, but I still yearn for my family deep down. They come to visit me, but only briefly, and then they depart.

I wonder... is Ethan waiting for me to come back to Lushbrook? Or has he forgotten me already? He used to ask me if I would ever forget him, and I said I never would. But what if someone else has replaced me in his life? He has so many people surrounding him—perhaps I am just a memory now.

Or perhaps… he still remembers.

CHAPTER 11

Waiting is the worst when you know the end is coming—when you know there's finally going to be someone who appears, someone you've longed for so desperately. Earlier, when there was no hope, when there was no sign that Izzy would ever return, I could lie by the river for hours, letting time trickle between my fingers like water. There was no restlessness, no patience—just the quiet acceptance of the unknown.

But this evening wasn't like that.

The night sky had grown dark, with indigo and violet tones that spread to blot out the remaining light over the horizon. Streetlights danced in the river with distorted and jittery reflections of light, looking as though a reflection of all the tumult brewing inside me. The sound of flowing water was soothing before but now sounded remote, lost amid the crashing cadence of my own heartbeats.

I looked back at the road for what felt like the hundredth time, my heart tightening in a strange expectation. She was close. I knew it. And that alone was enough to confuse me.

I had waited before in ignorance of when—if at all—she would return. But now that her return was certain, every second seemed like an eternity. The restlessness tormented me, a muddled mix of hope and anxiety seething within me. My phone vibrates once again—Alex's messages flashing on the screen, one by one—but I barely noticed. Nothing else seemed important at that moment.

The breeze carried the scent of damp ground, the remnants of a drizzle past, but even that was not enough to ground me. The world just went on as usual—cars speeding by, people smiling around there, the murmur of urban life in the distance continuing as if nothing was amiss.

Nothing had changed for everyone else.

When I finally decided to leave, my step slowed with unspoken thoughts, and a shattering screech cut through the night. My feet froze in their motion.

A car hurtled down the highway, tires screeching briefly before it slid to a halt outside a restaurant. My breath caught in my throat.

I knew that car.

And in that moment, everything else faded away.

Izzy.

She emerged, slowly walking, her eyes on the restaurant entrance. But she did not enter. She stood there, hesitating as if weighing something. I found it strange to look at. If she had intended to come here and have dinner, why was she just standing outside?

I paused for a few seconds before I went up to her.

"Why stand here outside?"

She didn't answer right away. Her eyes, far away and unreadable, locked onto mine, and for a moment, it seemed like she wasn't actually there, lost in thoughts far beyond my own. Then, in a flash, something changed in her face. A confidence I had never seen before emerged, bursting through like a sudden wind.

"Do you have money?" she asked, her voice bold, almost commanding.

The question took me by surprise. The Izzy I knew had been cautious, quiet, and weighed down. But today, she was different—blunt, fearless, unapologetic.

She tugged the hood of her hoodie down a bit, her fingers working through her hair as if rearranging it absent-mindedly. "Well?" she pushed, frustration dancing in her voice. "I'm starving."

"Uh… yeah, I have money," I said, still attempting to get used to this new twist on her part.

"Good. Let's go then." Without giving me time to say anything, she spun around and went into the restaurant.

For a moment, I just stood there, observing her. The way she walked today—there was no hesitation, no apparent burden on her shoulders. It was as if a part of her had been released.

I trailed behind her inside.

By the time we sat at the table, I allowed her to order. She didn't hesitate—noodles, sandwiches, pizza, ice cream... and the list continued. I was surprised. The Izzy I knew barely ate, surviving sometimes on dry bread. But today, no holding back, no second thought.

While waiting for food, she also looked around to take in the ambiance of the restaurant, sharp eyes surveying every inch of it. She then turned towards me, this time with a teasing grin on her face.

"Fascination over me, hmmm?" She asked with mock amusement, speaking in a feisty tone. "Falling in love already?"

Her words caught me off guard. I felt heat creep up my face as I turned away hastily. There was something about the way she said it—not just playfulness, but confidence, certainty.

How could a person change so much in a single day?

And yet... I couldn't find anything repulsive about it.

She sat there, laughing, chatting, eating with ease—entirely at home in this new incarnation of herself. And somehow, simply watching her like this was enough.

When the food came, she did not hesitate. She ate like she had not seen food in years, her hunger naked and unbridled. I sat quietly, watching her. This was the first time I had ever witnessed her eat so freely, without restraint, without reserve.

As we ate, I saw a few individuals in the restaurant looking in our direction. Before long, some came up to me and asked for photos.

I was hesitant, looking over at Izzy. Would she mind all the attention?

But she was too busy eating to even catch on.

Hesitantly, I agreed, snapping a few quick pictures and signing a few autographs.

Just as I sat down, a woman in the group caught sight of Izzy and complimented her, saying, "Your girlfriend is absolutely gorgeous."

Something within me awoke.

Girlfriend?

The term rang within my head, racing my heart. I faced Izzy, about to set them straight, but before I could speak—

"Thanks," she replied nonchalantly, not even looking up at her plate.

I stood there in shock.

Did she just agree?

"What's running through your head?" she asked in a still unemotional voice.

I found myself struggling for words. "What was that?"

"Did I say something wrong?"

"No, I just... didn't expect it."

She leaned to one side slightly, as though pondering. And then, with that same quiet conviction, she stated—

"Didn't you wait for me all these years?"

I caught my breath. "...Yes, I did."

She just smiled and went on eating. That smile—it unsettled me. It made my heart full but heavy at the same time. Perhaps because I had never thought that we'd be sitting here like this—as if nothing had ever been between us.

"Stop staring."

Her words jolted me back to reality. Perhaps I had stared at her for too long.

Attempting to change the topic, I said, "Why did you not go to the riverside today?"

She went quiet. The motion of her lips ceased. Then, after a pause, she faced me.

"Why? Did it have to be done?"

"...No. I was merely inquiring."

When we were done, she headed back to her car in silence. I stood there, my mind running over the conversation, word for word, look for look.

And then, just as she was getting into her car, she hesitated.

Turning back, she returned to me, closing the gap until we were almost touching. Her eyes had something in them—something unreadable, something intense.

"I'm here because of you," she murmured. "Remember that."

The air between us thickened.

She stepped closer, her breath warm against my skin.

"I'm interested in you," she whispered. "Or... you could say I'm in love with you."

Then, with a small smirk, she added, "Let's date."

She leaned in just a little more, her lips brushing my ear. Then, she winked.

I should have been over the moon. I should have felt like the luckiest man on earth.

But I didn't.

Instead, a strange sense of unease settled over me.

It felt... wrong. Like her words meant something other than what they seemed to.

So, I halted whatever was going on.

Laying my hands lightly on her shoulders, I pushed her back—just far enough to put some distance between us.

"Too late," I whispered. "You ought to go home."

She didn't stir for an instant.

And then, silently, she turned, slipped into her car, and disappeared.

And I just stood there, looking down at the empty street, wondering—

Who was this Izzy facing me today?

1st January 2016

Today, our caretaker, Mr. Brooks, got seriously hurt. It seems that he injured himself while working, and now he is in a very bad state. Due to this, Mom and Dad visited here, but when I requested them to take me along, they did so without hesitation.

I am so angry with Dad. He sent Sophia and me to Eldoria, far from all that we care about. He is still not taking us with him.

Sophia is even angrier than I am. She yelled at Mom and Dad, and Mom even cried. I didn't like that. But Sophia's actions were not right. When I attempted to speak with her, she just labeled me as weak and spineless and shut me up.

Perhaps she is right. Perhaps I am weak... because no matter how hard I try, I just can't fight back like she does.

CHAPTER 12

Since I met Izzy at the restaurant, an endless array of questions had started surfacing in my mind. I ought to have been elated to meet her, but a strange unease settled within me instead. The moment that I had never even dared imagine had now become a reality—yet, no wave of exhilaration swept over me.

Why did I not feel comfortable with her coming closer to me?

Why couldn't I even smile at her confession of love?

Why did an unknown fear, a suffocating unease, begin to take hold of me?

Fifteen years—so many years I had wasted just waiting for her. And now, when she had come back finally, when she had made that step forward and told me the truth, why was there turmoil within me? I should have hugged her, drowned in her eyes, but nothing of the sort occurred. There was something within me keeping me back—a wall that suddenly stood between Izzy and me, a wall that could not be seen but felt.

Ever since the night, I had unconsciously avoided visiting the riverside. Where I sat for hours day after day, muttering away to myself, drowning in the memories of her, where her presence had also lived on, even when she wasn't physically present—today, I wanted nothing to do with that location.

Was all this rushing past too swiftly?

Was I not ready to accept this truth?

Or was there something I had felt for Izzy that I did not want to admit?

I did not have answers. Only a profound bewilderment, extending its roots deep within me. I was on the set of the movie, shooting a scene, when I saw Alex speaking to a person. He would constantly look my way and, after some time, thumbed me up from a distance. I could not understand what it was—he was grinning. Upon completion of my shoot, I went a bit away and sat on a chair to rest.

Alex ran towards me.

"I have some good news for you," he announced with a wicked smile.

"What news?" I demanded, suspiciously eyeing him.

He pulled a chair in and sat down next to me. "You see that fellow I was just speaking to? He gave me that address," he said, handing me a piece of paper with an unfamiliar address written on it.

"You haven't taken your evening strolls these past two days, have you?" He put a hand on my shoulder, giving the impression that he knew something interesting.

"Just say it plain and simple—whose address is that?" came from my lips.

Alex chuckled. "The same girl you have been waiting for the last fifteen years. She sent it. She invites you over to her place. That means she is missing you."

He was thrilled, but after that night, my own emotions were all knotted up. Alex could have read my face because he scowled.

"Why do you look like that? What's wrong?"

"Alex, I am confused about her. The last time, when she tried to get near me, I pushed her, and..."

"What? You pushed her?" He glared at me. "Ethan, listen. You waited fifteen years for her. That's a long time. Don't let unnecessary thoughts get in the way of you two."

He was right. I couldn't stay away from Izzy because of some weird feeling.

"Don't let her slip away this time."

I nodded. I couldn't let her slip away now. I had waited fifteen years for her to come back—without really expecting that she ever would. Now that she was finally here, I wanted to make beautiful memories with her.

Grasping the address from Alex's hand, I climbed into my car and headed toward Izzy's place.

1st January 2018

Today, during an interview, Ethan said that he adores sitting on the riverside. The instant he said so, my thoughts flew back to that one day in Lushbrook—when he had taken me to the riverbank. I can still recollect how serene it all felt, how his presence made everything seem ideal.

I observe him daily. I have lost count of how many times I've watched his films and learned all of his interviews by heart. I even purchase all the items he sponsors, as if possessing them makes me nearer to him.

Recently, I've begun studying how to paint portraits—just for him. If I were to meet him again, I would present him with a portrait of himself, something I've created myself.

So many years went by. Perhaps he forgot about me, but I will remind him. I just need to see him once. Just once.

CHAPTER 13

When I first came across Izzy, I simply wished she would laugh and play along with the rest of us. But she was different—quieter, lost in her own universe. Unlike children our age, she never moved around randomly, and never laughed at jokes. As if she had an invisible burden, something that none of us noticed.

She had it all—a luxurious life that children like me could only imagine. And yet, she appeared unfinished. What had been done to her? What had transformed her into this state?

The next day, I visited her house to ask her out. It was the first time I had ever entered her residence.

No—not a residence. A mansion. An ancient haveli that had been standing for centuries.

Her family was among the wealthiest in the nation, but they came here only for a short holiday every year. As I entered, I caught my breath. Tall ceilings towered above me, the walls lined with paintings of those who'd lived here before. There was a sweeping staircase in the middle, leading up to the higher floors like something from a fairytale.

And then I saw her.

Izzy was coming down the stairs. Slowing. Swimming in elegance. For a second, she resembled a princess out of an ancient legend—regal, poised, but cold, as if she were of a place I might never be able to touch.

But she wasn't content.

She had an aura of isolation, a muted gloom that clung to her like a shadow.

She descended to the bottom of the stairs and beckoned for me to accompany her. We entered the living room, and there was an old woman seated—a woman with eyes that contained warmth. Izzy's grandmother.

She cradled a drawing book in her arms.

I was curious as to what was within it, but before I could query her, I greeted her.

"Hello, ma'am."

She smiled. "So you're Ethan, the boy who rescued Izzy the other day?"

I nodded. "Yes, ma'am."

She laughed. "Oh, son. Don't call me ma'am. Call me Grandma."

For someone who came from such a privileged background, she was surprisingly warm. Despite their wealth, they were not snobs. She summoned the servants and had them bring in trays of refreshments—so many that the entire coffee table was laden.

At the end of this, Izzy sat quietly, her head on her grandmother's lap, eavesdropping on our chat silently. Her fingers idly flicked along the top of the cover of her drawing book.

Later, her grandmother queried, "So, Ethan, what do you want to do when you grow up?"

I smiled, crunching down on a cookie. "A teacher."

Izzy's grandmother smiled kindly. "That's a commendable profession." She then spoke to Izzy. "And you, dear? What is your profession?"

Izzy had been keeping still, but now she moved, faltering. "Acting," she whispered.

Her grandmother stroked her fingers through her hair, a move so full of affection that it was obvious Izzy was fondest of her.

"So you want to act?" I asked, hoping she would finally say something more.

Izzy sat up, shaking her head. "No."

I frowned. "But you just said—"

"I enjoy that career. But I don't want to be an actress."

I was going to ask why, but before I could get the words out, her grandmother replied for her. "Izzy enjoys drawing. She wishes to be an artist."

I turned to Izzy, smiling. "Then will you draw a picture of me?"

She stared at me flatly before shaking her head. "I don't draw people."

I laughed, but there was something in her response that gave me pause.

With her grandmother's permission, I took her out to discover Lushbrook on my bike. Within five days, I introduced her to everything—the endless fields, the steep hills, the winding river, the bustling marketplace—every little nook that made this town unique.

And during those days, I saw something alter in her. She smiled. She laughed. At times, she even grew angry. Somehow, within a span of days, I had drawn out every emotion in her, making her feel a bit more alive.

Something that always tortured me was something she said when she left, the day before. We had sat on the riverside, the golden glint of the setting sun in her eyes, causing them to almost look delicate.

"Don't forget me, please." She had pleaded. But why?

"Fine, but if you promise me something as well."

"What?" she asked through her sadness and curiosity.

"From now on, you'll stay just like this—cheerful, fearless, and most importantly… confident." I added, "If you stay like that, I will never forget you." At that time, I just wanted her to be a cheerful child so I asked her to be.

CHAPTER 14

I was at the entrance of her residence—a huge mansion with high walls. From afar, I could already notice the giant trees towering over the property. I rang the iron-covered doorbell, and after a few seconds, an old servant opened the gate. When I asked to see Izzy, I was denied at first. But maybe my rep came in handy because, with a brief telephone call, I was let through. As I entered, my eyes landed on a lovely garden where some workers were working on the plants. A servant escorted me through the house to a waiting room, where a familiar face was waiting for me—Maya. The same girl who had taken me to Izzy by the river the first time. She was Izzy's assistant.

Maya invited me in and asked me to sit down. The size of the house was itself evidence that Izzy was from a rich family. This mansion used to be owned by her parents, but now it is occupied by her alone.

She told me that Izzy never received visitors to her house, but somehow she had consented to meet me. With that, Maya left to bring Izzy.

A few seconds later, I heard the sound of footsteps coming down the stairs.

It was her.

She wore a loose gray t-shirt and pajama pants, her hair messy, walking down slowly, almost precariously, as if she had been coerced into doing so. As she approached, the pungent smell of alcohol greeted me.

My heart dropped.

Izzy… like this?

I moved with slow, uncertain steps toward her before I dragged her into my arms. My hands shook as I enveloped her, and my heart thumped so hard that I was afraid she could hear it. I clutched her harder, feeling the fatigue in her frame, and the tiredness in her breathing. The anguish she bore was so real that it permeated me, causing my chest to hurt.

Time stood still. Words were not needed. All that was left was the bearable weight of feelings we both had suppressed for far too long.

Her breath was warm against my face, sending a shiver coursing through me. At that moment, it was us alone—the rest of the world had come to a standstill.

"I'm… I'm sorry," I whispered, barely able to speak. It was the hardest thing I'd ever said, but all that I could give. I clutched her closer, not wanting to release her, as if to release her would be to lose her once again.

Then, however, she pushed me away softly.

Her eyes contained a pain more intense than anything I had ever encountered. And another thing—fear. Why?

"Why are you here?" Her voice was soft but uncompromising.

Something within me broke.

"Izzy, what's wrong?" I stretched out for her hand, pulling her back in my direction. I couldn't lose her again.

"Please, don't do that," I whispered, my heart begging, my voice trembling.

Her gaze locked with mine, but the look was removed, inscrutable.

"Just go away. And never return," she said, and her voice carried no feeling whatsoever.

I felt a wave of numbness wash over my body. "But, you gave me your address," I whispered.

Her mouth curled into a wobbly, unspoken refusal, but then she shook her head. She looked away from me.

"Just listen to me," her voice was softer even now, as if she were begging.

"Go."

A single word demolished me. I felt the earth beneath my feet give way. I wanted to yell, to ask her a million questions, but I couldn't. All I could do was hold on to her once more.

"Don't do this, Izzy. Please." my voice cracked.

She didn't say a word. She just took my hand and walked toward the door. I didn't protest. Each step I took felt heavier—like my heart was being torn into pieces.

When we reached the garden, she stopped and gazed at me once again before she closed the door.

I remained there, overwhelmed with regret, shame, and pain. Perhaps she was upset with me. Perhaps being around me hurt her more.

I went down on my knees, questioning everything in my head. "What did I do?" "Why was she pushing me away when I knew—deep down—I knew she still needed me close?"

I remained there for what seemed like hours until the door opened once again.

This time, it was Maya.

"You must leave," she told me, her voice steady.

"But I can't leave her in this state!" I protested.

"You must," she said, and at her nod, the house staff moved toward me.

"You must stay away from Miss Isabella. It's for your own good."

Her words reverberated in my head. "Who did she think she was to determine what was best for me?"

I didn't care about what Maya believed. All I cared about was Izzy. I had read it in her eyes—she wanted me to leave, but something else was preventing her from doing so. Something she wasn't telling me.

I spent that evening in the garden, looking up at the stars like Izzy once did. It was odd… it felt as if I had lost something valuable and was desperately looking for a means of bringing it back.

Maya had attempted to shoo me away, but when I wasn't budging, she disappeared into the interior of the vehicle. She returned moments later—with a pillow and a blanket, this time. She put them on either side of me and smiled knowingly at me, with a hint of a smile.

As though she knew I wasn't moving anywhere.

That evening, I stayed out in the garden. Alone, with my own thoughts and Izzy's memories.

No matter how bad things were getting—"This time, I was not going to lose her."

15th August 2020

Every one of my duties has been taken over now by Uncle Andrew. Mom and Dad don't visit me anymore. I feel so alone... so totally alone.

School was over, college was over, and now Uncle Andrew has shut me up in this house. I am not permitted to go out anymore. I plead with him, beg him, but he doesn't pay any attention. He has even cut off all the telephones. Now, we are stuck here—prisoners in our own homes.

I don't get it. Uncle Andrew loved me so much before. What happened? Why is he doing this? If Aunt was the one being mean, I would have understood—she has always been like that. I never got along with her, and she never got along with me either.

Whenever she visits here, she quarrels with Sophia, and I detest it. I detest the way she speaks, the way she behaves with us, the way she behaves as if this house is hers. Why does she visit here? I simply don't get it. I just didn't get them doing this to us.

CHAPTER 15

As soon as my eyes opened, there she stood right in front of me. I got up fast, but the rush of guilt filled up my chest.

"Izzy, I'm sorry. Forgive me once, please, just that once. I will never do that again to you," I promised, my voice shaking.

"I don't know what happened to me back then, why I had that strange feeling," I continued, words I just couldn't hold in anymore, wanting her to understand.

"Please, just forgive me once."

I kept going on telling her I was sorry, non-stop, and all the guilt I had been carrying within me started spilling out. She just stood there, silently listening, with no expression on her face.

"Were you sleeping on that bench?" she asked softly.

I nodded, the remorse weighing inside me.

"Are you mad at me?" she said, quite coolly except for a delicate edge of weakness in her words.

Anger? How could I ever be angry at her? Even if she scolded me every day, I could never be angry. My heart was too pure for that. I knew she didn't mean to hurt me. Whatever happened was just a misunderstanding, an unfortunate moment that we both needed to move beyond.

I pulled her close to me without a conscious thought and hugged her in a tight hold. "Izzy, please don't ever leave me." My voice was whispery, barely above a breath.

She wrapped her arms around me and held me back. "Do you want me to always be by your side?" she asked softly, with an unsureness and hopefulness in her voice.

I nodded and could not utter more, but just let emotions overpower me. Then, at that moment, nothing else seemed to matter. I looked across the balcony when I saw Maya standing there. She was standing some distance, observing us, but it was irrelevant. It did not matter what anyone said or thought of us. Now, I had Izzy and would not lose her.

We entered inside. As soon as I stepped into the kitchen, I felt something was amiss. There was nothing in the cabinets. I wanted to cook something for her, but there was nothing. There was nothing in the fridge except some packages of bread and some liquor bottles.

I went up to Izzy, gently moving the hair from across her face, when I said softly, "You need to stop drinking."

She looked at me, and her expression was uncertain. "Are you trying to claim authority over me?"

"No," I said, my voice steady but firm. "I'm trying to free you from the pain that you are carrying inside."

With that, I picked up each bottle one by one and threw them into the sink. Izzy didn't stop me. She just watched silently, perhaps realizing that I wasn't going to let her live that kind of life anymore.

That was it. From now on, I was going to be the one to take care of her, to keep her safe from the things that hurt her, even if it meant making hard choices. I wasn't going to let her drown in her sorrow any longer.

On that day, we had breakfast together, watched a movie, had lunch, and even took care of the plants she had always been so fond of. However, something was different about her—her choices, her preferences. Still, spending time with her made me happy.

Maya, though, looked a little off. She was looking at us from that odd perspective. It wasn't just her. The house staff had an odd look in their eyes, as if everyone was subliminally watching us like something was off.

The doorbell rang.

Izzy didn't rush to open it. Instead, she took a slow breath, steadying herself. When she finally pulled the door open, Eleanor Thornton stood on the other side—poised, rigid, and exuding the aura of a woman who carried both wealth and entitlement like a crown.

"Hey," Eleanor, her aunt and Andrew's wife stepped inside without waiting for an invitation. Even her greeting was laced with condescension, her sharp gaze scanning the room as if Izzy didn't belong there.

Izzy didn't flinch. She stood up, meeting Eleanor's cold stare with an unyielding one of her own.

"You're still here?" Eleanor's tone was dripping with disdain, as if Izzy's very presence offended her.

Izzy's lips curled slightly, but there was no amusement in it. "What do you want, Aunt?"

Eleanor let out a dry chuckle, stepping closer. "There is nothing left here for you."

Izzy's fingers curled into fists. "I don't need anything from you."

"You've grown bold," Eleanor remarked, tilting her head.

Izzy took a step forward. "Why? Should I be afraid of you?"

Eleanor's eyes darkened. "You should leave. Go back to Eldoria. You're causing problems here."

The air in the room grew thick with tension. The unsaid words between them carried a weight neither was willing to drop first.

Before I could even process what was happening—

CRASH!

Izzy grabbed the vase from the nearby table and smashed it against Eleanor's head with alarming force.

"Izzy!" I shouted, stunned.

Eleanor staggered, her hand flying to her head. Blood seeped through her fingers as shock flickered across her face. For the first time, she looked genuinely caught off guard—as if she had never expected Izzy to retaliate like that.

Izzy was about to strike again when the household staff rushed in, grabbing hold of her before she could do more damage.

"Let me go!" Izzy struggled, fury blazing in her eyes.

One of the staff members quickly escorted Eleanor outside, her pristine white outfit now stained with crimson. Even as she left, she threw one last glare at Izzy, filled with seething hatred.

I just stood there, unable to move.

That… was Isabella Thornton?

The same girl I once knew?

The girl barely expressed her feelings, smiled, and barely talked back to people.

Now, she stood there with an air of recklessness, her lips slightly parted in something that almost resembled satisfaction.

A question echoed in my mind.

When did Izzy become that chaotic?

Maya took Izzy away to her own room, so I was sitting in the living room by myself. I got up and paced, going over and over in my mind everything that happened.

My attention was then captured by a drawer. It had been left half-open.

Because of habit, I stood to shut it. But before I could touch the handle, I noticed something caught inside.

Something small and known.

I drew it out slowly, my breath catching as I identified it.

The cat keychain.

The one I had given Izzy so many years before.

For a moment, my brain went blank. She still had it? All that later?

But before I could sift through the emotions washing over me, my eyes landed on something else.

In the drawer, hidden under a crumpled piece of paper, was a box of sleeping pills.

A lot of them.

My chest constricted. Someone had stashed them here—or she had.

I took the paper, hesitating. My fingers shook a little as I unfolded it. That was a blank paper that was used to conceal those pills.

Whatever it was, I knew one thing

Something was very, very wrong.

15th October 2022

Uncle Andrew has appointed a personal assistant for me. Her name is Maya Reed. She's nice, and the way she's been treating me is very courteous, but... I don't entirely trust her. Uncle Andrew's attitude toward me has been changing over the last few years in ways that make me nervous. Something here just doesn't feel right.

Sophia always defends me, always battles for me. But what about me? I can't even defend myself. If it wasn't for her, I don't know if I would have gotten this far... maybe I would have quit a long time ago.

This house suffocates me now. It feels like being in jail. Mom and Dad haven't called me at all. And every time I inquire about them from Uncle Andrew, he brushes it off, telling me they're busy or that they sent him to see how I am.

But I don't want him—I want them.

I can't stay here anymore. I have to return to Astravia. I must see Grandpa and Grandma, see Mom and Dad, see Ethan. I must explain to them that I miss them so much. I must make them remember I am still around.

CHAPTER 16

The night air was chilly on my skin as Izzy and I sat along the riverside. The golden colors of the sun setting cast a reflection off the soft ripples, creating a scene of peace. She was smiling—really smiling—as she stared at the water, a sight that was not common and made my heart feel less heavy.

But my conscience wasn't clear. The picture of the sleeping pills I had discovered in her home kept on nagging me. Why did she have them in such quantity?

I hesitated before inquiring, "Do you have sleep problems?"

Izzy diverted her eyes from the river and stared at me, her face serene but inquisitive. "No. Why?"

I looked at her face, searching for any deception, but she appeared to be truly unaware. If she did not need them, then why were they present? Part of me wanted to press on, to demand that she tell me what was going on—but I restrained myself. She was already carrying enough on her shoulders. I did not want to increase her load.

I would uncover the truth for myself.

So I switched topics. I began to discuss Lushbrook, about the day we met. I had assumed she would recall, but as she listened, I noticed confusion flash in her eyes. She didn't recall much.

Initially, that understanding hurt, but I pushed it aside. What did matter was that she was there now, sitting next to me.

And then, she laughed. A real, untroubled laugh.

It was warm but soft—the kind of laugh I hadn't heard in years. I pushed the pills, the questions, the fears aside. All I could do was stand there and stare at her, captivated by the way her eyes sparkled in the fading light.

She just stopped in mid-conversation and turned toward me. Our eyes locked, and for the first time in a long time, I felt calm.

"Start over," she whispered, her voice husky. "Forget everything that went before. Let's build something new."

A tiny smile pulled at my mouth. I took her hands in mine, holding them carefully. She winced at the contact but didn't move away.

"Why start over?" I whispered. "Let's just go on."

Her brows drew together. "But—

"I have no regrets," I broke in gently. "Not for the time we spent together, not even for the fifteen years I waited."

Her mouth opened slightly, but she didn't say anything. She put her other hand on top of mine instead, her touch tentative but reassuring.

Before she could speak, I added, "Even if I were able to turn back the clock, I'd still prefer to meet you. I'd still spend those seven days with you."

She dropped her eyes. "And if I hadn't come back at all?"

I let out a deep breath. "Then… maybe I would've waited forever."

But the fact was, I didn't need to. Because she was sitting there now, next to me, and that was enough.

"Just don't go again," I breathed.

She seemed to think a moment before querying, "Are you sure you want me to stay?"

"Yes," I told her instantly. "Stay here with me. Forever."

And for a fraction of an instant, it felt as if it were all I needed. River, dusk-filled sky, whispered leaves—everything else didn't matter next to the warmth of her body by my side.

But then I looked again.

Maya.

She was standing in the distance, partially hidden behind a tree. And she wasn't alone. A man stood beside her, whispering something in her ear.

A strange feeling settled in my chest. I had always found Maya… suspicious. And now, something about her presence—watching us, lingering in the background—felt off.

I turned back to Izzy. "Do you trust Maya?"

She immediately shook her head. "No. I don't like her."

I arched an eyebrow. "Why?"

Her face clouded over. "Because she is always saying I am going to disappear."

My gut knotted. "What?"

"She doesn't say it outright," Izzy confessed, her tone softer now. "But she makes these odd remarks, like… it would be better if I were not here. As if she is expecting me to disappear."

A shiver ran down my spine. "Did you ever tell your uncle?"

Izzy looked away. "I don't like him either."

"What? Why?"

She shook her head. "Just forget about them." She looked back at me, her lips curving into a small smile. "I'm here with you. And you're talking about others."

She was right. This moment was ours.

So I set aside my discomfort, wrapped my hand around hers, and held tight. Because no matter what secrets were hiding in the darkness, I wasn't going to let her slip away again.

20th April 2024

Sophia has transformed so much. She's arrogant, nearly ruthless. She doesn't think twice about hurting people, and sometimes... I'm afraid of her. When I told her to stop, she laughed and said, "If I don't fight back, people will always see me as weak."

She's always fighting, always making someone bleed. And me? She tells me to just stand back and watch, to remain quiet.

But I can't keep doing this. I don't want to remain here.

I managed to get in touch with Mom and Dad somehow. It wasn't easy, but I explained everything to them. Initially, Dad wouldn't believe me, but Mom... Mom convinced him. They're coming to pick me up from here.

I'm finally escaping Eldoria.

And when I do, I'm telling Grandpa everything. About Uncle. About Dad. About how they kept me locked up for years. They don't get to just walk away from this.

CHAPTER 17

I sat next to Alex on the movie set, leaning back in my chair and asking him, "I told you to look into Maya. What did you find?"

Alex didn't even look up from his phone. "I have a lot of work to do," he muttered. "I don't have time to clean up the mess you've been making these days."

I sighed. He was right—I was a mess. Skipping shoots, not showing up with notice, spending days off only to hang with Izzy—Alex, as my manager, was dealing with the fallout of all that.

But I couldn't care.

Izzy was aggressive, avoiding her loved ones—nothing at all like the girl I had remembered. All I wanted to do was take her back, bring her up, and remind her of who she was before the world tore her apart. I was ready to put my own life on hold for a few months if it was needed.

Little did I know how soon I'd lose control over everything.

I was supposed to meet Izzy at the river that evening. The shoot ran long, so I asked Alex to drop me off there. When we arrived, I saw something that made my blood run cold.

Izzy was standing near the water, arguing with Maya.

And they weren't alone.

A man was standing beside them with half his face hiding in the dim light. Something felt odd about the way he held himself, like he was constantly checking over his shoulder for someone.

I moved forward, then realized that before I could call out to her, he made a move on her.

In a matter of seconds, Izzy was grabbed from behind and injected with something in her neck.

"Izzy!" I screamed as I ran to get her.

She gasped, stiffening as she tried to fight, but in a few seconds, her legs buckled beneath her. She hit the ground.

"What in the name of God do you think you're doing?" I shouted at the top of my lungs into the night.

He turned toward me, eyes frigid and calculating. "Mind your own business."

Hell to that.

I leaped at him, fists flying. He staggered back, but I never got the opportunity to hit him again because Maya screamed.

And then more people came.

Men with their street dress. They stepped out of a car parked on the street. They pulled us and Alex back before we could get in our way. Maya and the man then threw Izzy into the vehicle as he held her under the arms.

"Let her go!" I struggled, my voice hoarse with desperation. "Maya! What the hell are you doing?"

She didn't even look at me.

The car door slammed shut, and just like that, they drove away, leaving me screaming her name into the night.

The men who had restrained us left soon after, getting into another car and disappearing down the road.

Alex and I took off in my car. Our only lead: Maya's car.

It brought us to the house of Izzy.

We parked, staying at a distance, but enough to watch how Maya's car pulled into Izzy's driveway. The housekeepers were quickly ushered out with Izzy inside, but it was more than them.

Her uncle was there, too.

When her uncle reached for Maya's hand to shake, my heart balled.

"What the hell is going on?" Alex mumbled.

I did not have any answer.

He had always been Izzy's uncle. But then why was he standing there, acting like he was a part of whatever just happened?

Was he the one behind it all?

I was just about to storm into the house when Alex grabbed my arm.

"Think before you act," he cautioned. "We do not know what is happening yet. We need to figure out the whole story."

Mentally, I felt really cold while Alex pulled out his phone, showing the screen to me. The private detective who he had hired to follow Maya obtained some new information. We drove back to my house, where David was waiting for us. David is a private detective and one of Alex's best friends.

Alex and I sat down on the sofa as David placed his laptop on the table, opening quite a few files and images.

"Maya goes to the hospital every day at the same time—she spends about an hour in the morning there. Then she can be seen often around Izzy's house, trailing her from afar. She also regularly visits a particular medical store and meets Izzy's uncle at his office almost daily," David said.

An inexplicable restlessness settled in my chest.

"Izzy's parents died in a car accident just two days after she had returned from Eldoria. She is the only survivor of the car accident. According to David, her uncle and Maya have been constantly in contact ever since. And one more thing—Maya isn't from that place. She is a foreigner. I couldn't find much about her past," David continued.

My head was spinning. I could still recall how, during our childhood days, when Izzy's uncle first laid eyes on her smile, he went ballistic. He demanded that I call him "Uncle" since he treated me like his family. Was it possible that the same man who, in the old days, cuddled her in his bosom now wanted to kill his little niece, Izzy?

"It's just a matter of property," Alex said. "Since her parents are dead, Izzy is the only nominee. Maybe her uncle does not want her to—"

I balled my fists up in my pockets, unwilling to listen to what he was saying.

"No," I said, shaking my head. "He loves Izzy like his daughter. He will not do that to her."

But the seed of doubt had already germinated in my mind.

28th April 2024

At last, I'm home. I'm out of Eldoria.

I can't even begin to describe how joyful I feel! It's like I can breathe at last. No more chilly walls, no more sealed doors—home.

The first thing I will do is greet Grandpa. And then... I'll find Ethan.

But will he even recognize me? What if he's forgotten me? It's been so many years. He has a whole life now. New people, new memories. Maybe I'm just a piece of his past he doesn't even think about anymore.

But I still possess the cat keychain he gave me. And his scarf—I've kept it all these years. I'll show them to him. I'll let him know how much I missed him. Every single day. Every single moment.

Now that I'm here at last, I won't let this opportunity pass. I have to see him.

CHAPTER 18

The air was crisp—the kind that brought unsettling silence. The doorbell rang out, the chime cutting across the stillness that reigned outside in that house. The grogginess I felt after last night's storm of thoughts stayed long enough for me only to step out of my room before Alex had already pulled the door open.

Izzy stood there, her face pale, lips pressed together as if trying to hold something back. At the sight of her, a jolt shot through me, and I acted without thinking: I closed the distance between us and pulled her into a tight embrace.

"You okay?" My voice was barely steady as I held her, my fingers clenching onto the fabric of her jacket like letting go would mean losing her.

"I'm fine," she whispered, but the way she clung to me said otherwise.

I drew back just enough to look at her, my heart pounding."Izzy... last night at the river... I saw Maya. And then your uncle. I think they're behind all of that."

The moment the words left my mouth, I felt her body stiffen. Her grip on my arms loosened as she took a small step back, her expression unreadable.

"You were there?" Her voice was hushed, laced with something between shock and fear.

I nodded, keeping a close eye on her. She just stared there for a moment, her eyes flickering back and forth as if trying to tally something in her head. And then, without warning, she grasped my hands harder than before.

"Ethan, forget all that. Just back away from my family. Back away from Maya."

The intensity with which she spoke sent shivers down my spine.

"What?" I furrowed my brows. "Izzy, we have to go to the police! You're in danger!"

Her fingers tightened around mine, but something else had come into her eyes now—something distant.

"No," she said, that time more firmly.

Alex, silent until now, stepped forward, his face serious. "Izzy, listen. That isn't just some family issue. Something's going on, and you know it."

Then her head snapped back, and her eyes went dark. "No!" Izzy cut through him. "You both get out of my way." Her voice was the sharpest thing I'd heard her say so far.

I looked at her and searched for some way in the expressions on her face to understand anything, but instead, I got desperate.

"Now, just believe me, okay, Ethan. Believe me, not anyone else."

It's as if those words were just a cold wave.

I want to believe in her. I want to put my trust in her, but how can I when everything just screams out and says that something is wrong, that she was pushing me away for reasons unknown?

That isn't just some family issue. It wasn't just grief, nor was it fear. That was something worse, something a lot more evil lurking beneath that surface.

Alex and I looked at each other, both of us thinking the same thing. Izzy wasn't just scared. She was terrified.

And then, when I thought things couldn't get any worse, she made one final request.

"If you want me to stay with you, then please do as I asked."

I felt my breath leave my body. "Izzy, what—"

"Please." Her voice was barely above a whisper now.

She was building a wall between us, shutting me out completely.

And I didn't know why.

As soon as she left, I had no intention of letting her go alone. I knew she needed me at that moment, whether she admitted it or not. By the time I reached downstairs, her car had already sped away. Without wasting a second, I got into my car and started following her.

She was racing as if desperately trying to save herself from some deep storm. I couldn't afford to miss her car for a moment and hence sped up. Leaving all the city-bright roads far behind, the deserted outskirts caught our sight, where a drizzling rain started trickling. Slick, these roads became a little slippery, wet.

At that time, there was her stop in front of a beautiful bungalow. I had seen that place before, the magnificent Thornton family estate. Its splendor was evident from afar. The massive iron gate slowly opened on its own as if obeying an unseen command. I knew gaining entry here wasn't easy, but at the moment, nothing was stopping me. Sensors at the gate of the villa recognized Izzy's car and the doors automatically opened. I went into the garage with my car without a moment's hesitation, but she didn't seem to notice that either.

It was in the early morning hours, but the garden of the villa seemed quite busy. People were watering the flowers while house staff cleaned and dusted, and some lady was decorating the entrance by piling some pots with beautiful flowers. Soft sunlight was kissing the white marble to make that whole place shine more radiantly.

Avoiding all attention, I went in. The living room was grand and regal. Huge glass windows allowed morning light to pour into the space. The chandelier was not lit, but a deep silence filled the room and added to the elegance. The family seated inside had already been greeted by Izzy. All turned towards her, their faces etched with concern due to the fact that Izzy looked at them with anger.

I would remain still in the corner, trying to comprehend what was happening. Izzy stood in the middle of the room with her fisted hands and tensed body. Her grandparents were seated on a sofa but the expression was unable to be read. Maya and Mr. Andrew were standing next to her, apparently seriously talking.

Izzy's sharp step forward cut the air. Her voice hollow, with irritation ensued.

"Why can't you all just leave me alone?" she hissed, her gaze flitting back and forth among the faces that filled the room.

Her words fell like a stone into still water, dropping a heavy quiet into the space. Her grandmother's hands were shaking slightly as she reached to take her husband's, then grasped it tightly, holding on for security. Her fear was palpable, but for what?

The uncle's voice sliced through the silence, chilled and unforgiving.

"Why don't you just leave instead?" he said, his tone carrying an unmistakable edge.

I furrowed my brow, thinking. Leave? Was he asking her to return to Eldoria? But why now?

The air in the room became even more oppressive. Izzy's breathing had increased, her shoulders rising and falling as she felt anger burning just beneath the surface of her skin.

No sooner had her uncle's words escaped his lips when he shouted once again, louder this time.

"Don't you come near Ethan. Don't involve him in all that. You hear?"

I opened my eyes wider. His words seemed to sink inside of me as though he told her to get away from me.

A shockwave of shock lanced its way through my being. Why?

At the party, he had been the one who made it possible for me to see her at the party. Now that he supposedly had a problem with me, why had he allowed it all to happen? And now that Izzy and I had finally found our way back to each other, why was he all of a sudden trying to pull us apart?

I clenched my fists tightly at my sides, trying not to move.

They knew. They all knew how much I loved her. I had never hidden it. So why was I suddenly not good enough?

"Waw!! Now you care about your niece?" Izzy's voice dripped poison as she herself burned with fire.

"Ethan doesn't belong to you," her uncle said. The next second she grabbed at her uncle's collar, and her hands began to shake—not out of fear but out of rage and betrayal.

"Izzy, stop it!" I jumped forward to catch her shoulders and yank her back.

Her breath came in short gasps, and her body tensed, but she froze for a second.

The room was heavy with stifling silence. Everyone watched me.

There were questions in their glances—Why was I there? Why was I standing alongside Izzy?

But Izzy didn't give a damn. She moved forward, reached out, and gently touched my cheek with her quivering fingers. Then she said,

"Just believe me, Ethan... everyone in that place lies."

Something was unnerving in her gaze—resolution, anger, and something else, something I did not get at all.

I kept staring and told her immediately, "I trust you."

Before I could get another word out, her uncle's voice rang out,

"I need to tell you something, Ethan."

I had no idea what he was going to say, but before I could utter a word, Izzy sprang into action.

She wheeled around, snatched something from the fruit basket on the center table, and spun back around in one fluid motion.

A knife shone in her hand.

My heart thumped.

"Izzy, what are you doing?" I asked, my panic rising in my chest.

She pressed the knife against her uncle's throat.

The whole room froze.

"Stop that madness! Let go of the knife!" Maya screamed.

But Izzy's face didn't change.

"Why? Why can't you all just leave us alone?" she screamed.

I was completely lost.

Izzy had always been closer to her uncle than to her father.

But now... now, he was the one she wanted to hurt.

Had she found out about some kind of betrayal?

Or... maybe it wasn't about that at all?

Then, Maya's voice thundered, loud and clear—"Sophia, stop it!"

I stood still.

Sophia?

She called her Sophia.

Why?

Izzy's hesitation was used.

And in that split second, her uncle took advantage of the situation.

He pulled a syringe out and plunged it deep into Izzy's neck.

"No!" I screamed, but it was too late.

Izzy's face screwed up in pain before her body started to weaken, and her eyelids began to droop.

Her grandparents' eyes filled with tears.

I stood there, frozen, and couldn't really process what was happening.

Why were they doing that to Izzy?

Who the heck was Sophia?

And what the hell was really going on?

1st May 2024

My parents are dead. And Sophia… Sophia has turned into a monster.

She's hurting others. And deep down, I know—I just know—that she was involved in my parents' murder. The mere thought sends shivers down my spine. What if I'm next?

I pretend to be fine. I attempt to put her to bed, to calm her down. But the reality is, I'm scared. What if she attacks me? What if she attacks the rest of my family too?

I don't want that to happen.

I tried to kill her many times but I failed every time.

I've kept her from having proper food anymore—just bread. I get rid of all the rest before she can get her hands on it. Maybe if she weakens, then she won't be able to hurt anyone any longer.

I instructed her to leave today. She would not leave. Rather, she frightened me into silence.

I am trapped. Helpless. Alone.

Mom, I need you. What am I to do?

Should I just do what Justin did…?

CHAPTER 19

Maya and some of her people took Izzy upstairs, leaving me to sit on a bench under a tree in the garden. Beautiful trees and blooming flowers surrounded me, and in the middle of the garden stood a marvelous fountain. My eyes were stuck on the water falling, and I was in deep thought.

My mind was full of thousands of questions, and I had no answers. First, I thought Maya and her uncle wanted to hurt Izzy, but everything seemed different now. Her grandmother was crying, and her grandfather was trying to console her. I had no idea what was happening with Izzy. Why had Maya called her Sophia? Why did it feel like I didn't know my Izzy at all?

Distracted by my thoughts, I barely felt my phone vibrating. Alex's message appeared on the screen: Are we canceling today's plan too? I typed a quick "Hmm" and stuffed my phone back into my pocket. Then, once again, my eyes wandered back to the fountain, with the sound of falling water echoing the confusion in my mind.

"Help me?"

Snap out of that, I refocused on the water feature, just as Maya settled beside me. My thoughts were already plentiful, and in seeing her sit there, those questions had not diminished.

Looking at her is where I now sought answers.

"You must have a lot of questions," Maya said, correctly interpreting my confusing expression.

She was right. I didn't know what was going on. A few weeks ago, I was almost sure that Maya and her uncle wanted to murder Izzy. Now everything seemed so different.

"Tell me the truth." My voice sounded stern, but inside myself, I wasn't sure whether I wanted to hear it or not.

Maya crossed her legs and let a deep breath out, "I'm a psychiatrist. I've been treating Izzy for the past two years."

Those were words like a shockwave. A psychiatrist?

"Why? What happened to her?" I asked, my voice full of concern and disbelief.

Maya hesitated before answering, "Izzy has Dissociative Identity Disorder. In other words, she has two personalities. One is Izzy, the girl you know. The other... is Sophia."

She made me stare blankly at her, trying to process what I had just listened to.

"How do you have two personalities?

Maya took a slow breath and continued, "Dissociative Identity Disorder occurs when the mind of a person creates another identity to cope with something painful—something they cannot handle alone. It mostly occurs in people who undergo deep trauma, especially at a young age. Their minds create a different version of themselves to protect them. That is what happened with Izzy.

"Izzy... created Sophia?" I whispered, trying to understand.

Maya nodded. "Yes. Izzy is quiet, gentle, and reserved. But Sophia… Sophia is strong, aggressive, and unafraid. Izzy made Sophia fight for her—because Izzy herself couldn't fight back."

My chest began to clench. I suddenly realized why everything was making sense.

At that moment, everything became clear.

Why I felt nothing when she walked away, and sometimes meeting her eyes could make mine well up with tears.

Why do her expressions and words sometimes feel mismatched?

Why, when she asked me to stay, something deep in her eyes silently begged me to run.

Why, at times, her closeness felt suffocating, even when I had longed for her presence.

Izzy was right.

My heart had always recognized her—even when my mind failed to understand.

That was Maya's voice cutting across my thoughts.

"How long has that been going on?" I asked

"More than fifteen years," she replied, the gravity of her words weighing down my bones. "Several psychiatrists have tried to work with her before me."

I gulped hard. "So why isn't she any better yet?"

"With time, Sophia is slowly taking over Izzy, and Izzy is retreating somewhere deep inside," Maya said, her voice laced with concern.

I turned my gaze from the fountain and looked at her. My mind was filled with countless questions.

"How can I help?" I asked.

Maya placed a reassuring hand on my shoulder. "Because you can control Sophia. I've noticed she's not aggressive toward you. You can reach Izzy."

"The issue is that Sophia is slowly assuming full control of Izzy. That is termed Identity Alteration where an alter becomes increasingly dominant to the host personality. Izzy discovered that whenever Sophia takes control of her, she becomes vicious. That's the reason why she has come up with Psychosomatic Weakness—that she subconsciously made herself weak and frail so that Sophia would not have enough force to do damage to people around her.

"Did she do that on purpose?"

"Not exactly. But she is suffering from Self-Induced Fatigue and Dissociative Amnesia. She takes high doses of sleeping pills to remain asleep, repressing as much of Sophia as she can. But by doing so, she is also deteriorating her own body and brain."

I crumbled into a million pieces of heart when I heard that.

Izzy had been putting up with such a lot without my even being aware of it.

And now... I finally understood what she had meant that night.

Look into my eyes. That is how Izzy looks at Ethan. Never forget that.

She was trying to tell me who she was.

She was trying to make me see the difference between Izzy and Sophia.

She was asking for help.

But I hadn't understood.

And now... it might already be too late.

"Sorry, Ethan, we didn't tell you earlier." Izzy's uncle exited the garden into the lawn area, his eyes filled with tears of remorse.

"That is the reason we could never tell much about Izzy before... Please forgive us."

I shut my fists into tight balls to prevent my words from bursting open. "Until now, I couldn't do anything for her... but promise me, bring my Izzy back."

Mr. Andrew's hand on my shoulder calmed me down, and his words felt heavy and deep. "Thanks, Ethan." Tears welled up in his eyes as Maya helped calm him down.

28th May 2024

I've barricaded myself in this house with Sophia. I don't allow anyone to see her, but there is one person I want to see—Ethan.

Nothing ever happened between us—no relationship, no vows. And yet, I could never forget him. What began as friendship has now evolved into something more, something that I can no longer deny. But fear clutches my heart—what if Sophia injures him?

Every evening, after I put Sophia to bed, I walk down to the riverside, hoping to catch a glimpse of him. But it's been days, and I have not seen him, not even once. Will I ever catch a glimpse of him again? Will he ever remember me? Or have I already slipped out of his memories, just like time has forgotten so much in mine?

CHAPTER 20

We had taken Izzy back home from her grandparents' house, where we were staying. She was lying in bed, and I sat down next to her, holding her hand lightly. The white curtains over the window near us danced with the breeze and let sunlight fill the room. It was a room that always felt dim, but today, I had opened all the windows, and light filled the space, illuminating the place where she had spent so much time in darkness.

My mind was consumed with one question: When she opens her eyes, will it be Sophia or will it be Izzy?

I kept watching her peaceful face, brushing the strands of her hair away.

I had never seen Izzy that close again—too close, too warm. I'd never thought I could have such a chance at ever seeing her in that lifetime. She was like a princess to me, almost inaccessible, one that loved could only dream of and even meeting just kind of felt like a meant-not-to-find outcome. Yet fate had given us some days together, a brief friendship... though for me, those days would last a lifetime.

I never let anyone else enter my life. Maybe it's because my heart never accepted anyone else. And honestly, I never tried. I waited for Izzy—without hope, without expectations. I knew, deep inside my heart, that she would never return. And yet, my heart never stopped calling for her.

But that day… as I sat by her bedside, I felt like I was holding the whole universe in my hands. She was right there—so close, so real. I could see her, feel her presence, and in that moment, I wanted nothing more than to freeze time and live in it forever.

I was waiting for her to wake up. For her to open her eyes, to look at me, and maybe… just maybe, for her to still be the Izzy I had always loved.

It had already been two hours, and I hadn't even noticed. Time had slipped through my fingers like it didn't exist. Izzy's uncle had told me to go home, but how could I? All I wanted was to see her, be near her.

So, over the last few days, I had met her many times, spoken with her, but... those conversations weren't really with Izzy. Those meetings weren't really with her.

Then, she came to slowly open her eyes, twitching them sideways. The light of the room made her squint. She instinctively lifted the hand I was holding across her eyes. I wanted to help her sit up, and just as my hand moved in that direction, she pushed herself up, speaking,

"What are you doing here? Leave."

Her words cut through me, sharp and sudden. At that moment, I wanted to see... was she Izzy or Sophia? But the moment our eyes met, my heart answered for me—it was Izzy.

She hadn't even gotten a word out of her mouth when reaching out for my wrist and pulling me down the stairs. Down in the living room, Maya, Mr. Andrew, and the household staff, who, by coincidence, were nurses, looked up when they heard the commotion. Their eyes followed as Izzy dragged me down, and the moment we reached the bottom, she tossed both myself and her uncle out of the house.

I stood there, confused, unable to understand why she was doing that. Why was she pushing me away?

Mr. Andrew and I walked to the garden and sat down in silence. For a while, neither of us spoke.

Finally, I turned to him. "Mr. Andrew, why is Izzy pushing us away? I don't understand anything."

His answer was quiet but firm. "Because she doesn't want Sophia to hurt anyone."

My breath caught. "Has Sophia... hurt someone?"

Mr. Andrew only nodded. Before I could ask anything else, his phone rang. He answered it and left, leaving me alone with my thoughts.

31st May 2024

Today, after fifteen long years, I actually saw him. Ethan. Sitting on the riverside, just as he would sit. My heart skipped a beat—I had imagined this day a thousand times, but now that it had arrived, I was paralyzed. I wanted to rush to him, shout out his name, inform him how much I had missed him. How each and every day, I had thought of him. But I just sat next to him quietly, fearing that if I spoke, the moment would break. He didn't even seem to notice me at first, just continued to stare at the river, deep in thought. Did he remember me at all? Did I still live somewhere in his mind, or had time completely erased me?

CHAPTER 21

During the shoot, I had a small accident. It happened during a stunt scene—I lost my balance and fell hard on the ground. At first, I thought it was just a minor injury, but when a sharp pain shot through my arm and my left hand went numb, I realized something was seriously wrong. People rushed toward me, and within minutes, I was taken to the hospital.

Now, I found myself lying on a hospital bed with my cast-wrapped left arm and, in addition to it, on my forehead rested a light bandage. Here sat Alex concernedly, smiling all the way to try to brighten up.

"Dude, the doctor said your hand won't be able to move for another fifteen days."

I took a deep breath and stared at the ceiling. "I can't stay like that for fifteen days. I have too many things to do."

Alex raised an eyebrow and smirked. "Oh, I can guess what those things are—Izzy, Izzy, and only Izzy!"

I tried to laugh, but the pain made me wince instead.

"Stop making me laugh," I muttered.

Alex chuckled. "I hate seeing you like that, but get yourself together. Izzy needs you."

Just then, the door opened, and Maya walked in. Her face was tense. She took one look at me and quickly approached my bed.

"Oh God, you got hurt badly!" she said, her voice filled with concern.

I shook my head. "Don't worry, it's nothing serious."

Maya gave me a doubtful look. "It doesn't look like 'nothing' to me."

"I'm fine, Maya," I said firmly.

"Are you sure you can still help us in that condition?"

I looked into her eyes. For a moment, I forgot about my injuries.

"If it's for Izzy, I can do anything."

Maya gave me a small smile, but she still looked worried.

Just then, Mr. Andrew walked into the room. He glanced at me before speaking in a serious tone—

"Thank you, Ethan. We are grateful for what you're doing for us."

I gave a small nod. The truth was, I wasn't doing that for them. I was doing that for Izzy.

Andrew took a deep breath before adding, "Izzy made the best decision of her life when she chose you to be friends with you."

Hearing that, a faint smile appeared on my face. But deep down, I felt uneasy. I knew Izzy's situation was far worse than they realized. Sophia had completely taken over her mind.

Maya's voice turned serious. "Alright, Ethan, as soon as you feel a little better, we'll begin."

I took a deep breath and nodded.

"Done. Leave it to me. I'll go see her tomorrow."

Maya and Mr. Andrew left, but Alex was still staring at me.

"Tell me honestly—did you break your hand on purpose? So you can take days off," he asked, giving me a suspicious look.

I quickly shook my head. "What? No way! It was just an accident. Who in their right mind would break their hand? You're overthinking."

Alex and I were back home, but my mind was still back at Izzy's. I couldn't be still—I needed to go back to her.

As I moved toward my bedroom to change clothes, Alex detained me.

"Ethan, not today. You need to rest for a couple of days."

I looked back at him with a sorrowful face. "How can I rest when she's in agony by herself? I can't make her continue suffering."

Alex sighed, worried in the depths of his eyes. "I know, but your state—"

"It's not as bad," I interrupted him, pushing aside his worries.

Swept by his words aside, I ventured into the closet in search of attire. But with only a functional hand to guide me, even something so elementary as that became a test of endurance. Irritation fermented in me as I struggled to make sense of the fabric, incapable of working without assistance.

A few minutes later, Alex came in, his face etched with worry.

"Let me help you," he said, extracting my clothes and helping me dress. His hands were firm, but his voice conveyed unspoken concern.

"Take care of yourself, Ethan. I'm worried about you."

I leaned my head lightly against his shoulder. "Don't worry, I'll be okay."

Alex took me to Izzy's house. I lingered for a second outside, my heart racing.

Who would I see today? Izzy… or Sophia?

Whichever it was, I knew one thing for sure—my mission was to return Izzy.

I went into her bedroom and opened the door slowly without creaking. She lay on the bed with her eyes focused on the chandelier from the ceiling.

The windows of her bedroom were shut, and there were no lights on. The only source of light was faint and sneaked through the curtains to give the room a gentle mist.

She remained there, silent, her eyes staring at the ceiling. Her eyelids were rimmed with unshed tears—her eyes were wet, but the tears just refused to fall.

She was my Izzy—the one who could lose herself.

My heart hurt to see her like that. When you love someone, their hurt slices through you more deeply than it slices them. And that is what I was experiencing.

"Izzy," I whispered.

She slowly turned her head to me, her gaze locked onto mine. And then the tears she had stored all that while finally started to flow.

Her eyes seemed to be saying a silent message to me, *I need you.*

She just continued to look at me, not able to speak, but her tears told everything. My eyes too brimmed with tears seeing her tears.

I crept up to her, but she didn't move—she just stood there staring at me.

"Don't approach me," she whispered, shivering. But her eyes… her eyes implored me to remain.

Please… don't abandon me.

I sat next to her, brushing away her tears, although my own continued to fall. My hand ran softly through her hair.

"Why don't you just leave me?" she whispered, her voice cracking.

"If you wanted me to stay away, then you shouldn't have returned to my life," I asked while patting his head.

"I missed you... I just wanted to see you." Her words came from her heart. Her eyes were locked with mine.

"Do you think I never missed you?" I asked, my voice shaking. "I missed you even when I thought you'd never return. And now... now, how can you tell me to release you?"

"I'm sorry, but you don't get it, Ethan."

"Then make me get it."

"I could hurt you."

"I don't care. Just don't lose yourself trying to push me away."

"Why can't you get it?" she begged.

"Because I don't have to know anything other than that—I'm not going anywhere."

She sat up in bed, now turned towards me. With both of my hands clasped in hers, she stared directly into my eyes. "I'm not the same person you knew, Ethan. Everything has changed."

"You haven't changed. You're still you. Believe me."

I just needed to make her stay. I needed her to bury Sophia deep inside forever. But we had to make her believe that we needed Izzy.

"You know nothing."

"I know one thing for certain—I love you."

She began to pull her hands out of mine, but I gripped them harder. I couldn't let her leave me.

"Even I despise myself... why can you possibly love me?" she whispered, her voice shaking.

"I don't know... I just do."

She started to sway, her body losing equilibrium. Her eyelids blinked, fighting to remain open.

"Izzy!" I grabbed her just as she fell, setting her down on the bed. Panic flooded my system as I pulled the blanket over her tiny body. My fingers touched her icy forehead before I gently retreated.

That's when I noticed the bedside table.

A pill bottle. Almost empty.

My breath was caught in my throat. A queasy realization settled in.

She wasn't only fighting Sophia. She was injuring herself to stop her.

8th June 2024

He returned to the riverside after a whole week. He was so calm, so innocent-looking. Did he know who I was? If not, why did he say, "Have we met before?" Perhaps he was just being polite. How could he possibly remember me? It's been 15 years, and I've changed so much. There's no way he still remembers me… right?

I miss Grandpa. Maya informed me that he wishes to meet me at the hotel party. I am nervous… What if Sophia harms him? She no longer listens to me. I somehow succeeded in putting her to sleep, but for how long? I don't know.

The thing is, I'm afraid. What if she finds out that I'm feeding her sleeping pills to render her weak? What will she do to me? And more so… what if she discovers Ethan? If that were to happen, and she attempts to harm him... what will I do?

CHAPTER 22

Alex and I strolled through the imposing lobby of the Grand Regent Hotel, our footsteps resonating off the gleaming marble floor. The smell of fresh flowers and high-end cologne hung in the air, combined with the muted hum of voices. We approached the elevator in silence, our heads burdened by the upcoming conversation. The silver doors opened with a smooth glide, and we entered. The ride to the top floor seemed like an eternity.

Mr. Andrew Thornton's personal office was on the top floor, surveying the whole Grand Regent kingdom. The entire floor belonged to him—exquisite, imposing, inaccessible. And yet, standing here, I was agitated, restless, as if crossing into taboo areas. My heart pounded faster as the elevator went up, the numbers flashing one after another until we reached our destination at last.

The receptionist shot us a knowing look before pressing a button on her console. A moment later, she gestured toward the double doors behind her. "He's waiting for you. Go on."

Alex and I shared a look before advancing. The thick wooden doors swung open into a huge office, filled with the warm light of the afternoon sun streaming through the floor-to-ceiling windows. The panorama was stunning, but I hardly saw it. My attention was on the man sitting behind the enormous mahogany desk.

Andrew Thornton's presence was as authoritative as ever. His expensively cut suit was spotless, his silver hair slicked back, and his piercing stare carried the authority of a man who had made hundreds of hard choices. But today, there was something more in his eyes—something guarded.

I didn't dawdle. "I need to discuss Izzy."

His fingers drummed against the shine of his desk before he invited us to sit. We sat, and for a moment, there was only silence between us. Then, he leaned forward, his face inscrutable.

"What do you want to know?" His voice was controlled, but it was weighted.

I looked up at him; my throat parched. "How long has she been like that?"

For the first time, his mask cracked. A shadow flickered across his face, quickly but unmistakably. He breathed softly before he spoke.

"She wasn't always that way," he said softly. "It all began when her older brother had committed suicide—right in front of her. She was only twelve."

My breath froze in my throat. "Her brother... Justin?"

Andrew nodded, his jaw clenching. "Yes. Izzy loved him. But when he died, everything changed. She quit speaking. She'd sit in the dark recesses of the house for hours, not moving. And then, occasionally, she'd get violent—out of control."

I balled my fists. "When I first met her, did she already have that illness?"

"Yes," Andrew acknowledged, his voice laced with something akin to regret.

I breathed out, my thoughts reeling. So it had begun all those years ago.

"That's why you sent her to Eldoria, didn't you?" My tone was softer now, the gravity of understanding settling in my chest.

Andrew's jaw clenched. "Yes. Because Izzy had withdrawn far inside herself, and Sophia had taken over completely."

A shiver ran down my spine. Sophia. The name itself was ominous.

"Did Sophia ever hurt anybody here?" I asked, though, in reality, I already knew that she did.

Andrew nodded sternly. "Yes. We began to receive complaints from her school. It became apparent that she wasn't safe around other people. That's why we sent her away—to a private facility, out of the public eye. She had medical supervision there."

I glared at him, shock flooding my face. "You sent a twelve-year-old girl away, by herself? Did you consider what she was going through at all?"

"It was necessary."

"Her treatment could have been done here! Why Eldoria?" I shouted, my voice escalating. "She was battling all of that by herself!"

Andrew returned my glare with an expressionless face. "We didn't want people labeling our Izzy crazy."

A bitter laugh escaped my lips. "So that's why you never told me the whole truth?"

Andrew sighed, rubbing his face. "I didn't want anyone to know."

Fifteen years. For fifteen years, she had been suffering, and I had been totally oblivious.

"But why isn't she better yet?" My voice was gentler now, the anger gone, replaced by sorrow.

Andrew hesitated before speaking. "Because Izzy doesn't want to let Sophia go."

I stood there, frozen. "Why?"

He turned away, as if the words themselves were too painful to speak. "I don't know."

There was silence in the room. The only noise was the far-off tick of a clock, each tick drawn out interminably.

"After her parents died, she would not see anyone. She barricaded herself in her apartment. She hardly eats—just booze and sleeping pills."

I gulped hard, my stomach knotting. "Why is she doing that to herself?"

Andrew's face darkened. "Perhaps she's weakening herself—so Sophia won't be able to hurt anyone else."

An oppressive silence followed. My heart was being squished by the weight of everything.

Then Alex suddenly spoke up.

"I will help too."

I turned to him, surprised. He had said nothing the entire time, allowing me to speak. But now... he was volunteering to assist?

Alex was always trying to keep me out of trouble. He was always cautioning me when I was too emotional. But now, even though he had no personal stake in Izzy, he was going to assist her.

I looked at him.

He was serious.

I nodded, resolve settling in my chest. "Then let's do that."

Because no matter what it cost, I was going to get Izzy back.

20th June 2024

Sophia learned about Ethan. That evening at the party, I learned that Ethan never forgot me—he had been looking for me all along. I was thrilled. I believed everything would be okay now, that we would be together forever.

But now Sophia knows, and she won't even let him approach me.

I'm afraid. She's moving in on him. She told me Ethan would be with her before he'd ever be with me. She warned me to go away if I didn't want to watch him suffer.

If going away keeps Ethan safe, then perhaps I should do this. I couldn't possibly beat Sophia—she's too strong. But at the same time, I'm not going to just let everything go like this.

CHAPTER 23

The cool night air wrapped around us like a soft, silent blanket as we gazed up at the starry sky in Izzy's garden. The darkness above was endless, stretching far beyond what the human eye could comprehend, while the stars twinkled like distant whispers of forgotten memories. The world felt still, almost as if it were holding its breath. Beside me, Izzy remained quiet, her gaze fixed on the heavens, lost in a realm of her own thoughts.

I shifted slightly, propping myself up on one elbow as I watched her, unable to tear my eyes away. There was something about the way she was so absorbed in the night that made her seem distant, unreachable. The soft glow of the moon illuminated her features, casting delicate shadows across her face. She looked peaceful in the stillness, but I knew better. Beneath that tranquil exterior, there was a storm brewing. It was a storm I couldn't understand, and yet, it was one I couldn't ignore.

I turned my head, staring at her as if waiting for her to speak, to say something—anything—that would help me understand what was going on inside her. But she didn't speak. She just lay there, her eyes locked on the sky as if searching for something beyond it.

Then, as if sensing my gaze, she turned her head toward me. Her eyes met mine, and I felt a shiver run down my spine.

"What are you looking at?" she asked, her voice soft but sharp, as though it carried an undercurrent of something I couldn't place.

I hesitated, my heart suddenly racing. The unease in my chest grew heavier, threatening to swallow me whole. There was something different about how she spoke—something that felt unnatural. I took a deep breath, trying to steady myself before responding.

"Leave her alone," I said, the words tumbling out before I could think twice. I didn't even know where they came from, but they felt necessary. The moment I said them, I knew they were for Sophia, the other side of Izzy that had been lurking beneath the surface for far too long.

Izzy's face shifted, and for a split second, I saw it—the darkness. Her eyes, once warm and filled with vulnerability, now seemed colder and distant, as though they belonged to someone else entirely. The smile that crept across her lips was cruel, twisted in a way that made my stomach churn.

"What do you mean? Who should I leave alone?" she asked, her tone laced with amusement. It was the kind of amusement that sent a chill through my bones—the kind that didn't belong to the Izzy I knew.

I forced myself to hold her gaze, my throat tight with fear. "Izzy… leave her alone," I repeated, my voice shaking but determined.

There it was again—the shift in her expression. It was subtle but undeniable. The eyes I was looking into were no longer Izzy's. They were cold, calculating, full of something darker, more menacing. They were Sophia's eyes, and for the first time, I could feel the weight of her presence bearing down on me.

She looked at me for a moment, and then, in a voice that was dripping with cruel amusement, she said, "Oh… so you've finally figured it out."

I nodded slowly, trying to keep my voice steady. "Yeah. I know now. Just let her go."

Izzy's—no, Sophia's—smile widened, stretching across her face like a mask of evil. "She needs me," she said, the words oozing with something sinister.

"She has me. She has her family," I countered, the desperation creeping into my voice. My heart pounded in my chest as I felt the weight of those words—the truth of them—but they felt so hollow, so insufficient in the face of what was really happening.

"Family?" Sophia repeated, her voice dripping with mockery. "Family," she said again. This time laughing bitterly, the sound echoing in the night air. She sat up abruptly, and I followed her, my body stiff with unease. "If they cared even a little, I wouldn't be here."

I could feel the cold sweat on my brow as I sat up, my heart hammering in my chest. "I know, but I'm here. I'll take care of her. Just... just let her go."

Sophia's eyes darkened, and she leaned in slightly, her face mere inches from mine. "Forget it, Ethan. She's never coming back."

My breath caught in my throat, cold dread creeping into my bones. "W-What do you mean?" I stammered, my voice trembling with fear. "What are you planning to do to her?"

Sophia's eyes lingered on me, a consideration of whether I was worth an answer. Then, finally, she said, her voice low and detached. "I don't have to do anything. She is already killing herself."

The words hit me like a physical blow. My stomach twisted in agony, and for a moment, the world seemed to tilt around me. "What?" I whispered, disbelief clouding my thoughts.

Sophia let out a quiet laugh, devoid of any humor. "After returning from Eldoria, she tried to end her life. More than once."

My heart stopped. My breath became shallow, my hands trembling as I struggled to process what she was saying. "No… no, that's a lie," I whispered, shaking my head in denial. "That's impossible."

Sophia tilted her head, her smile widening. "A lie? Really?" she scoffed. "She believes I killed her parents, Ethan. And now, she thinks I'll hurt you... and her family. So she is thinking of killing me; that means she has to kill herself."

I shook my head, trying to push the words out of my mind. "No, she can't kill herself. She will have to kill you."

Sophia studied me for a moment, her gaze piercing, before answering in a soft, almost indifferent voice. "Why do you care so much, Ethan? We are the same person. It shouldn't matter to you."

The words hit me like a punch to the gut. "You are not Izzy!" I snapped, my voice raw with emotion.

She smirked at me, a knowing look in her eyes. "You know, I could do anything to her. And you wouldn't be able to stop me."

"Please," I begged, my voice cracking. "I'm begging you... just let her go."

Sophia's expression softened, just slightly, and she stared at me with something almost... sad. "She created me, Ethan. And you're also part of the reason why."

The world tilted beneath me. "What are you saying?" I whispered, shivering. "Are you telling me Izzy made you? Because of me?"

Sophia's smile returned, but it wasn't cruel that time. It was known, almost as if she were savoring that moment. "Think back, Ethan. What really happened in Lushbrook?"

The question lingered in the air, heavy with unspoken truths. Then, without another word, she stood up and walked back toward the house, leaving me sitting there, my mind racing, my heart pounding in my chest.

What had I done back then? What had I done that made Izzy need Sophia?

June 21, 2024

I don't think my disappearance will make any difference. I'm not going to let Sophia have Ethan. I will protect him. I will save him from her. After what she did to my parents, I won't let her do the same to Ethan.

I've made up my mind—I know what I have to do to protect my entire family.

Grandpa, Grandma, I miss you so much, and I love you.

And Ethan… I'm really sorry. I love you more than anything. I just want to ask you one thing—please remember me. Remember the good things about me. And no matter what happens, please don't ever hate me.

CHAPTER 24

The soft light of the morning filtered through my curtains, but my eyes still felt heavy with sleep. Just then, I heard a knock at my door, loud and urgent.

"Ethan, open the door." Alex's voice came from the other side. His tone was different—sharp, tense, and filled with a kind of urgency I'd never heard before.

Bewildered, I rubbed my eyes and pulled myself out of bed, still hardly awake. Opening the door, I found Alex standing there, his phone held in front of him. His face was one I couldn't quite identify—concern and a touch of panic.

"What's going on so early in the morning?" I asked, my voice hoarse with sleep, but the worry in his eyes made my heart skip a beat.

"You need to see this," Alex said, his voice shaking slightly as he handed me his phone.

On the screen was a news headline that made my stomach drop: **Thornton's Only Heir Turns Herself In. Late Night Confession: She Killed Her Parents and Is Now in Police Custody.**

My head felt like it was spinning. I blinked rapidly, trying to comprehend what I had just read, but the words were blurry as if my mind couldn't catch up with the shock.

I glared at Alex, hardly above a whisper, "What is this? Why she…"

He didn't respond immediately; his eyes widened, as though looking for some indication that he was mistaken. "I—I don't know, but we have to go. Now."

I felt a cold chill run down my spine. There was no time to think. I couldn't understand why Izzy would do that, why she would confess to such a terrible thing. But there was no time for questions. I quickly grabbed a jacket over my nightwear, and without a second thought, I followed Alex out to the car.

As the car sped through the streets, I attempted to understand it all. Why on earth would she do that? I kept asking myself. Why would she take the blame for something like that? The distance to the police station seemed to stretch on for a lifetime while my mind was filled with unanswered questions.

By the time we finally reached the station, my pulse was racing. The media were out in force—camera lights, microphones, reporters screaming questions as they mobbed the entrance. The gravity of the situation sank in. Izzy was not any ordinary person. She belonged to the most influential family in the nation. The press had already gotten wind of the news, and that would be a public spectacle.

Alex pulled the car to a stop, but I could already feel the pressure mounting.

"There's too much media here," he warned, his grip tightening on the steering wheel.

"I don't care," I said firmly, my voice steady despite the chaos outside. "I'm going in. Now."

Alex sighed, then gave a cap and mask to me. "I'm not stopping you, but just, be careful."

I nodded, not sure I could trust my voice to say anything more. I pulled the cap low over my eyes, adjusted my mask, and got out of the car. The cold air slapped me in the face, but my thoughts were elsewhere, overwhelmed by the commotion before me. We rushed inside, the din of flashing cameras and shouted questions receding behind us as we entered the building.

Inside, the tension was palpable. I spotted Izzy's family—her grandfather and uncle—standing in a corner, surrounded by a team of lawyers. The expressions on their faces were grim. My heart sank when I saw them. How could this be happening?

"She's admitted it, Ethan," her grandfather said, his voice shaky with grief. "She says she killed her parents. And now she's in police custody."

I couldn't manage to speak. There were no words available that could be used to explain that. I just nodded, the gravity of the situation crashing down on me.

"We need to get her out of here," one of the lawyers insisted. "We need to talk to her, to get her released."

"But how?" asked another lawyer. "She confessed. That's a serious charge. There's not much we can do."

I was in a daze, seeing it all happen around me but unable to make sense of it. My head was reeling. The reality of it all didn't seem like reality.

And then, as if the room couldn't quite take the awkward silence, Maya appeared. She hurried in, looking stern.

"She won't be going to jail," Maya said firmly, but with a calm tone. "Izzy has a personality disorder. She's mentally ill. She can't be treated as a criminal."

The room fell silent. I stood still there.

"What? You're telling me that's the reason she confessed?" one of the lawyers inquired, his tone acidic.

Maya nodded. "Yes. Perhaps her sickness made her think that she was guilty, though she's not."

Izzy's grandfather, who'd held it together until then, lost it. Sobs streamed down his face as he collapsed into a chair. I sat beside him, not sure how to help or what to say to him.

"Don't worry, Grandpa," I said quietly, putting a hand on his shoulder. "Everything will be okay. We'll fix that."

His voice trembled as he looked at me, his eyes filled with regret. "I wasn't a good grandfather, Ethan. I failed her."

I shook my head. "You've been a great grandfather. You've done everything you could."

He pulled me into a hug, holding me tight. We both stood there for a long moment, overwhelmed by the weight of what was happening, both of us grieving in our own way.

CHAPTER 25

The courtroom was thick with silence, choking on its quiet. Each breath, each pulse, seemed to reverberate against the walls as the judge rendered the verdict.

"The defendant, Isabella Thornton, is not guilty of killing her parents."

The words ought to have been freeing, but they instead left a hollow pang in my chest.

The proof was irrefutable. The CCTV footage on the night of the accident had finally revealed the truth—Izzy had been lying unconscious in the back seat of the car. She hadn't driven. Neither had her other personality, Sophia. For a month, she had carried the intolerable burden of thinking she had murdered her parents, but in fact, she had been an innocent passenger in a catastrophe that was out of her hands.

But even with her innocence established, her battles weren't yet done.

The word of her Dissociative Identity Disorder (DID) had gone viral. All the major news networks, and social media platforms, had labeled her the "heiress with a broken mind." Her mental illness had been turned into a spectacle, something to be argued and dissected.

The court, in recognition of her fragile condition, issued its final verdict:

She would be kept in a Psychiatric Rehabilitation Center until she was stable enough to be reintegrated into society.

The words hung like chains around my chest.

I turned to glance at Izzy. How did she take that?

She was gazing straight ahead, her face inscrutable. But then, slowly, slowly, her lips quivered. And before I could even think what was going on, tears started streaming from her eyes.

Izzy, who never showed emotion, who hardly even allowed people to touch her, was falling apart, right before everyone's eyes.

She didn't cry out loud, didn't scream. She just sat there, shaking her shoulders, tears trickling down her face like raindrops on delicate glass.

Since her parents' deaths, she had been locked in the prison of her mind, believing that she was a monster who had killed the people she loved most. She had punished herself, hurt her own body, and borne guilt that had gradually suffocated her.

But today, that weight had been removed.

And she could finally breathe.

For the first time in so long. I noticed something in her eyes that I hadn't noticed before.

The girl who always attempted to harm herself—that was the first time she indicated that she wanted to live.

Alex and I stood by the door as the medical staff were about to lead Izzy away to the Psychiatric Detention Center. I was numb, as if the fact of what was occurring hadn't sunk in yet.

I had waited years for her return.

And now, after I had finally found her again, she was being taken from me.

I saw her leave the courtroom, two of our staff surrounding her. She wore soft restraints on her wrists, but loose enough to loosen them and have to refasten them as needed—insurance to protect herself from doing something she didn't want to. She appeared so… diminutive. Breakable. Shattered with any pressure at all.

Would she disappear without seeing me? Like before.

Would she even glance at me?

And then—she did.

Her eyes rose, locking with mine from afar. Neither of us moved for a moment. And then, she motioned for me to step closer.

My heart was racing. I had braced myself for silence, for space—for her to depart without a word. But now, she was inviting me in.

I didn't hesitate.

I bridged the gap between us in a flash, holding her close.

She didn't struggle.

She was cold, as though life had been sucked from her; she didn't shove me away. She surrounded me with her arms, her fingers clutching the back of my coat as if she were reluctant to let go.

Neither of us said a word.

The world around us grew fuzzy—lawyers, journalists, police officers. None of it made a difference. It was just her and me.

Then, after what seemed like an eternity, she eased back.

Her eyes, tear-stained, locked with mine, and in a voice so low that I barely heard it, she breathed,

"I want to tell you something."

I nodded. "I'm listening."

Her mouth opened slightly as if she were looking for the words. Then, taking a breath, she spoke,

"I don't think I need to tell you this, but... still... wait for me. I'll return to you."

Some part of me curled up in agony.

I wanted to believe her. So much.

I manufactured a tiny smile. "Even if you don't, I'll wait for you."

A flash of something inscrutable went across her face. Then, after a moment, she breathed,

"But… if I'm too late, don't wait for me."

My chest constricted. "That's my choice, not yours."

"Let's start over when I'm back."

I smiled. "Why start over? We will continue."

"But…"

"I have never regretted a single moment I lived for you."

Her hands shook ever so slightly on my sleeve. She was struggling to be tough, but I could see the fight going on inside her.

"I have another favor to ask."

"What is it?"

"Until I am completely recovered, don't come visit me," she whispered, her voice shaking.

I gulped hard. "Izzy....but..."

"Promise me."

I ached to say no. To fight for her. To promise her that no matter what, I would be there.

But gazing into her eyes, I saw—that was something she required.

So I agreed. "Okay."

Her shoulders slumped as if she had been breathing in. Then, without another word, she turned and climbed into the waiting car.

The door shut behind her.

And like that—she was gone.

I stood there, still, my fists balled.

I didn't even know that my eyes were stinging until someone put a hand on my shoulder.

Alex.

"Why did you promise not to see her?" he asked quietly.

I gave a dry laugh, shaking my head. "Because if I kept seeing her, it would be even more difficult to stay away."

Alex took a breath, watching the car recede down the road. "You waited fifteen years for her. Why is that tougher?"

I hesitated. Then, after a long silence, I whispered,

"Before... I never expected she'd return."

I swallowed hard, my voice barely above a whisper.

"But now... I do."

And somehow, that hope made it so much more difficult.

CHAPTER 26

It had been a year since Izzy went away. But each day without her was the same—an incomplete day, an incomplete night.

I had buried myself in work, from one shoot to the next, from one meeting to another. My life was hectic—script readings, promotions, interviews… Everyone thought I was okay.

But when the cameras ceased to film, when lights were extinguished, and everything was quiet, the reality unfolded—I was all alone. And in that loneliness, Izzy was always there in my mind.

Each night, when the day was over, my feet moved automatically to one location—the banks of the river. It had become a habit. I'd sit there for hours, seeing the rippling water, but my mind was consumed by Izzy's memories. At times, I'd murmur to her, as though she could still hear me. At other times, I would just sit and remember her smile, her eyes, and the night she walked away from me.

I missed her every day. But I had sworn an oath.

I would not look for her. I would not contact her.

If she were supposed to come back, she would do it in her own time.

And so, I waited.

Even a year later, the world hadn't moved on from Izzy. The press had kept our names in the news, perpetuating constant rumors.

Ethan Rivers' Secret Romance Revealed!

Who Is the Enigmatic Girl?

A Superstar and a Billionaire's Daughter—Love or Scandal?

Others had made up their minds. Some described it as an untold romance; others simply wrote it off as a whim. But I never felt like I needed to justify.

For the truth was easy—Izzy had meant something to me. And I didn't mind what the rest of the world thought.

Curiously, no one had misinterpreted me. Those who understood me had caught the reality of my silence—my friends, my co-stars, even my fans.

Even Alex, who tended to avoid emotional subjects, had stood by me throughout.

One evening, when I came home, I discovered him sitting in the living room, typing away on his laptop. The moment he saw me, his fingers slowed, and he looked up.

"Are you okay?"

I had understood what he meant.

"Why are you asking?" I had said.

"Just asking."

I remained silent for a moment before responding, "I'm fine."

Alex hadn't been believed, but he hadn't pushed.

Rather, he'd asked something unexpected.

"If she never returns, will you keep waiting?"

I hadn't needed to ponder.

"Even if she returns on the day that's last on my calendar of life, I'll remain joyful."

Alex had blown out between his teeth, shoving his hand through his hair. "That girl doesn't realize how lucky she is."

He slumped against the couch, massaging his forehead as he grumbled, "People of this world have long forgotten love; they cheat on it, but you... you're waiting."

I smiled weakly, without bitterness.

"Love isn't being together, Alex. It's about making another person happy over yourself."

Alex had rolled his eyes. "Alright, let's stop it! It's getting too intense, and I feel uncomfortable."

I grinned. "Getting emotional?"

"No, I just—argh, forget it!" He had taken a pillow out of nowhere and slammed it onto my head.

I was surprised. "Did you just—"

Thud!

By the time I was able to react, he had hurled another one.

And like magic, the stifling atmosphere was gone. That dark, clammy night of the previous night had transformed into pillow fights and teasing. The last few minutes, we were children again—tossing pillows at each other, avoiding behind the sofa, evading blows.

And when we collapsed back onto the couch, winded, Alex had smiled. "You punch like an idiot."

I chuckled. "And you fight like an old man."

Leaving me aside, he had straightened up. "By the way, tomorrow there is an event at the Grand Regent. Get ready."

I nodded just like that. "Alright."

"Good. Now go to bed; you look drained."

Yawning, I responded, "Yeah, yeah. Goodnight, Alex."

"Goodnight, Ethan."

But when I had eventually made my way to my room and gotten into bed, the silence came back. The emptiness. The hollowness.

A full year had gone by. And I still didn't know what had happened to Izzy.

Was she all right?

Had she gotten over me?

And the biggest question of all—was Sophia still pulling the strings?

Those questions haunted me every day, eating away at me from the inside out.

But I had waited.

Because true love didn't disappear with time.

And I knew one thing for certain...

One day, she'd be back.

CHAPTER 27

The vehicle cruised down the streets of Veridale, familiar to us both, the city lights flashing against the tinted glass. Alex was behind the wheel, drumming his fingers idly on it, but I could sense him looking at me out of the corner of his eye. I had not spoken a word the whole way, my thoughts elsewhere far from the place we were going.

We were going to the Grand Regent.

A spot I had gone to countless times in the last year—each time with some excuse or another. Events, meetings, or a casual drive-by to catch up with her family. But the reality was that every trip was a quiet pilgrimage. Every entrance into the spacious halls made me remember her, and every word with her family made her absence ring even louder.

I always gravitated toward the garden.

That very garden where I had last seen her.

I would sit on the bench, running my fingers over the grain of the wood, gazing up at the moon and pretending—just for an instant—that she was sitting next to me, gazing up at the sky the way she always did.

"That is how Izzy looks at Ethan. Remember that."

Those words had lingered with me. Haunted me.

For so long, I did not know what they were talking about.

But now?

Now, I did.

She had loved me, always. In her own cracked, silent way, she had loved me with a kind of love that I had been too stupid to see.

As we approached Grand Regent, I sat by the window, my mind drifting back to that night—the chill of the wind, the shaking of her voice when she spoke, the look in her eyes as if she was grasping a secret she could never utter.

We stopped at the imposing entrance.

The warm light of chandeliers poured out into the great windows, lighting up the walkway that led indoors. Something cozy about that site, and also something heavy, which I never could shake away.

Alex slid the car into the park and unbuckled his seatbelt.

"Wait there," he told me. "I have to park properly."

I hardly replied, my attention already on the garden.

The evening was uncannily like the night a year ago. The same gentle wind, the same silver moonlight, the same muted murmur of activity within the hotel, and silence outside in the garden. The fairy lights danced along the hedges, sending fine patterns of light and darkness dancing over the stone path.

I moved forward, attracted by the spot like a moth to a flame.

The bench was unoccupied.

I slowly exhaled, ruffling my hair with my hand, and sat.

The wood was cool against my palms.

The air was filled with the smell of fresh dirt and jasmine that bloomed during the night.

I leaned back on my head and gazed up at the sky.

The moon was full that evening.

"Beautiful, isn't it?"

A low voice whispered from behind me.

I stiffened.

My breath caught.

The world around me seemed to fade into silence.

I slowly turned around, not wanting to shatter the moment if I moved too quickly.

And there she was.

Izzy.

Standing before me under the light of the moon, her dark hair falling over her shoulders, her eyes full of something I couldn't define. A soft smile spread across her face as if she had been waiting for me to turn.

I couldn't move.

I couldn't talk.

I simply gazed at her, wondering—was that real? Was she really here?

Or was that merely another cruel deception my mind had played on me?

She inched a little closer, and before I could do anything, she raised a hand and set it lightly on my shoulder.

The heat of her touch destroyed whatever barriers I had constructed within myself.

Tears swelled in my eyes before I could stop them. A trembling breath escaped, and then—

The dam broke.

I dropped my head, shoulders shaking as silent sobs wracked through me.

A year.

An entire year of waiting, aching, wondering if I would ever lay eyes on her again—

And here she was.

"Hey… what's wrong?" Her voice was soft, her fingers tightening ever so slightly on my shoulder.

I still couldn't find my voice.

She sighed softly and sank down onto the bench beside me.

Then, without a word, she leaned forward and wiped the tears from my face, her fingertips light as a feather against my skin.

"I'm here now," she whispered. "And you're still crying?"

I gave a broken laugh, shaking my head.

"I missed you." I finally got out, my voice barely above a whisper.

She smiled, that same little, knowing smile.

"Okay," she whispered. "Let's go inside."

"No."

I reached out, enfolding her in my arms before she could pull away.

"Not yet."

I buried my face against her shoulder, taking in her scent, feeling the heat of her pressing against me.

"Just... don't move like that."

She lingered for only a moment before her arms encircled me too, her hands pressed against my back.

For the first time in a year, I was able to breathe.

"Hey man, everybody's waiting. Let's go inside."

Alex's voice broke the tenuous moment.

I jerked away, wiping away the last of my tears.

And then I saw—

Alex was not surprised.

He wasn't shocked to see Izzy here.

That was when it registered.

There was no party.

That was all her doing.

She had wanted to surprise me.

And Alex? He knew all along.

I turned on Izzy, and she merely smiled, her fingers wrapping with mine.

"Come on," she whispered.

She took me in, our hands still intertwined.

The dining room was full of warmth and laughter.

Her whole family was there, and the instant we entered, they made me feel like family.

I hardly caught their hellos and hardly paid attention to the chatter around me.

Because all I could think about was her.

The smile she gave me.

How she gazed at me, no longer lost, no longer troubled.

Maya, who stood by her side, finally said, "Izzy, you're okay now... that makes me really happy."

Izzy's eyes met mine before she responded.

"I had to be okay," she said in a whisper.

Then she wrapped her hand tightly around mine.

"Because now, I have a reason to be okay."

I gulped.

For the first time in so long, there was no hint of sadness in her eyes—only love.

She walked me to the table with her grandfather. The entire family was in high spirits, with laughter in the air.

But me?

I was still clutching her hand.

I hadn't let go.

Perhaps…

Perhaps I was scared.

Scared that if I let go, she'd disappear all over again.

"So, Ethan… what are your plans now?" Mr. Andrew asked.

I looked at Izzy.

Then, with a slow, knowing smile, I turned to him.

"Should we go to Lushbrook?" I asked.

Andrew smiled. "Of course! Our Izzy is back—let's go!"

Then he turned to Alex and Maya. "You two should come too. You've done so much for us."

The dinner went on, full of warmth and stories.

And me?

I was still holding Izzy's hand.

And for the first time in forever—

I felt like my waiting was finally over.

But at that time, I had no idea that in Lushbrook, I was about to discover something that would completely change my story.

CHAPTER 28

The afternoon sun bathed Lushbrook in a golden glow; its warm light stretching across the quiet hilltop where my house stood. A soft breeze rustled through the trees, carrying the scent of wildflowers and damp earth. From up here, the town spread out below us, its rooftops glistening under the fading light. It was peaceful—just as it had always been.

Izzy and I were outside my home, swathed in a solemn quiet. Unspoken memories weighted the air between us, an unspoken aura that seemed to cling like ghostly impressions of a history that I was not yet fully familiar with. I looked up at the twisting road that wound its way up the hill, the corner of a nostalgic smile tickling my lips.

"Remember?" I gestured down the street. "That's where we met. You were walking down the street in the rain, soaked to the bone."

Warmth in my tone, the warmth that came from fond memories. But Izzy smiled softly and shook her head.

"No," she said quietly. "That's not where we met."

I furrowed my brow, taken aback. "What? What do you mean?"

Had she forgotten, or was I getting it wrong?

Before I could say another word, she grasped my hand. Her fingers were warm against mine, a welcome contrast to mine, which had gone cool in the chill evening air. I just stood there for an instant, gazing at her—her deep, wise eyes, the soft certainty on her face.

"Come," she said softly. "I'll show you."

With not a word, she took me down the winding, slanting path into the town below. The birds had started to roost for the night, their distant voices mixing with the creaking leaves. The sunbeams filtering through the trees created the dappled effect and the long shadows along the trail.

We arrived at the little market, where the air was filled with the smell of just-baked bread and flowers. Izzy took a slower pace as we approached a tiny flower shop, its wooden sign creaking softly in the wind. Next to it, a weathered, old bench sat under a vine of ivy.

She halted and gestured toward it.

"We met here, three years before that rainy meeting," she breathed.

I gazed at the place, my eyebrows furrowed in puzzlement. "Three years? I… I don't know."

Izzy smiled, but there was a wistful look in her eyes. "You were standing over there with your four friends," she said, pointing to a place by the shop entrance. "You had five pieces of candy. When you saw me sitting alone, you gave me the last one."

I racked my brain, but my memories were blank.

"You were the first person to ever give something to me," she went on softly. "In school, everybody used to take from me—take my things, anticipate gifts—because my family is wealthy."

Her words were even, but I sensed the magnitude of them. I never really had thought anything about it, but to her, it had mattered.

She took me deeper onto the path and this time I went without hesitation.

We arrived at the riverbank, where the water glimmered in the afternoon light. The sound of the current flowing over the rocks filled the air, just as it had always done. She gestured toward the thin path along the water.

"I was going for a walk here one day when you passed by with your friends," she whispered. "My laces were undone, and I had no idea how to tie them. You ran back and tied them."

A harsh breath shot out of me.

"So... you knew me the whole time?" I whispered.

She nodded. "I always wanted to speak with you," she confessed. "Since then, I always waited for June so I could come to Lushbrook, see you, and meet you."

For three years, she had quietly observed me from afar.

"You were a good person," she whispered. "You did things for people without asking for anything in return. I needed someone like you in my life."

A knot came into my throat. "Izzy… why didn't you ever tell me?"

She paused, then breathed deeply.

"I hunted for you," she confessed, her voice shaking. "The day you found me in the rain, I was stalking you. But I lost my way in the forest... and somehow, I ended up close to your house."

The understanding came to me in a flash. "So that's why you—"

She nodded. "Yes. I wanted to locate you. I missed you every day in those 15 years."

I gazed at her, amazed.

"I saw every film you ever played in, every interview, every commercial," she went on, a sad smile playing on her lips. "I wanted to return to you. But I was afraid."

I swallowed hard. "Afraid of what?"

She sighed, tears brimming her eyes. "That you'd not recall me. That I was simply an erased memory in your history."

Those words shot pain right through me.

"When my mother and father fetched me home from Eldoria, I vowed that I would search you out." She paused on the brink of more emotion and controlled it enough that it just missed spilling tears down her face. "Then… they disappeared."

Her mother. Her father. They're dead.

A heavy silence fell between us, punctuated only by the sound of the water lapping over the rocks.

Izzy broke it. "You spoke in a number of interviews about always finding peace along the riverbank."

"So that's why you'd come here over and over?" I asked, my voice barely above a whisper.

She nodded, her eyes fixed on mine. "Just to see you. To know you were safe."

A knot materialized in my throat.

This wasn't my tale.

It was hers, too.

She had always stood by—waiting, watching, clinging to recollections I had allowed to pass through my fingers.

Tears clouded my eyes, and when I glanced at her, I saw the same in hers.

"I didn't know you," I whispered, guilt invading my tone.

But Izzy shook her head, a gentle smile on her lips.

"It didn't matter," she replied softly. "Because I knew you were waiting too."

And in that instant, I knew—

I'd never been alone in my story.

I thought I knew her. But the truth was, she had always known me.

I thought I loved her. But the truth was, she had always loved me.

And I just never saw it.

"That love was never one-sided."

– Ethan.

9 789369 547

Printed by Libri Plureos GmbH in Hamburg, Germany